KNOWLEDGE FROM WHAT?

THEORIES AND METHODS IN SOCIAL RESEARCH

Derek L. Phillips
University of Amsterdam
The Netherlands

RAND MCNALLY COLLEGE PUBLISHING COMPANY • Chicago

Rand McNally Sociology Series
Edgar F. Borgatta, Advisory Editor

Current printing   (last digit)
15 14 13 12 11 10 9 8 7 6 5

FOR PATRICE

Preface

Although this is a small book, there are a large number of persons whom I wish to thank for their help and criticism. Among my colleagues and friends at New York University, appreciation is due to Alan F. Blum, Kevin J. Clancy, Irwin W. Goffman, Richard Maisel, Vanderlyn Pine, Richard Quinney, Gerald Rosenblum, William Silverman, and especially Eliot Freidson and Herbert Menzel. Special thanks are owed to Sanford G. Thatcher of the Princeton University Press and Robert A. Scott, Department of Sociology at Princeton, both of whom generously provided long and detailed comments on the manuscript—even though they knew I had decided to publish with Rand McNally. Needless to say, none of these people is responsible for what I have written. In fact, some strongly disagree with my point of view and my conclusions, and none approves of the manuscript in its entirety. Nevertheless, they have helped me enormously.

I also wish to thank Larry Malley and Stella Jenks of Rand McNally who helped see this book through to publication.

Derek L. Phillips

New York City
January, 1971

Table of Contents

Introduction

This monograph grew out of my dissatisfaction with the state of sociology as it is practiced on the contemporary American scene. Other sociologists, especially younger ones, have also expressed unhappiness with the present state of the discipline. While many of us share these feelings of dissatisfaction, it seems likely that this view has been reached from a variety of different experiences and via several alternate routes. Because it may be informative to learn how someone comes to question many of the beliefs, assumptions, and world-views that he has acquired as part of his training for membership in the sociological community, I intend to utilize this introduction for setting out some of the sources of my own doubts and to relate these to the eventual writing of this book.

In a book that raises many questions about the so-called objectivity of sociological research, it seems almost obligatory for me to provide some biographical information so that the reader can better understand my vantage point in doing this book. For it is my belief that, despite protestations to the contrary, the writer is always present in his narrative. I fully agree with the recent statement by Christopher Lehmann-Haupt (1969:23), book-review editor of the daily *New York Times*, who asserts:

> I find that more and more I demand to know exactly who it is
> that is talking to me. I want to know all about him. Why is he

> interested in the subject he's discussing? Does he under-
> stand himself well enough to know why? Was he there when
> it happened? Who told him what? Under what circum-
> stances? . . . Who are you to be telling me what you are
> saying now?

This, then, is a brief chronological recounting of how I came to
hold my present views (which are made explicit in the following
chapters) and to write this book.

While a graduate student at Yale, I learned about many of the
central concerns of sociology: culture, social structure, norms,
socialization, deviance, values, stratification. But what was considered most important and crucial to my training was the acquisition of knowledge concerning sociological theory and methodology,
the relationship between the two, and their respective roles in
empirical research. Certain "gods" were held up as exemplars of
theoretical purity (Parsons, Merton), methodological sophistication
(Lazarsfeld, Hyman), and research expertise (Lipset, Coleman). I
learned that one's hypotheses emerge from some systematic consideration or review of the writings of other sociologists, that these
hypotheses have some theoretical justification, and that they must
be tested empirically. I also was taught that sociological investigators are, and should be, value-free, and that a researcher's
theories and findings become cumulative. Finally, I acquired the
belief that most of our empirical results bore some rather obvious
relation to reality—to what is "out there." In short, I fully accepted
the views of those who saw sociology as an empirical and theoretical science. To state it another way, I internalized the dominant
paradigm (Kuhn, 1962) of the sociological profession.

For several years, these continued to be my views. My lectures
in introductory sociology at Wellesley and Dartmouth always contained some allusions to the ways in which sociology resembled
other sciences. And my own empirical investigations were predi-
cated on the assumptions that there was general agreement as to
what constituted good research, and that such research would
make a positive contribution to the discipline. During the first few
years after obtaining my doctorate in 1962, I was engaged in studies
of public attitudes toward the mentally ill, the causes and distribu-

tion of mental illness, happiness, and illness behavior. My convictions at that time are reflected in the introductions to two books which I edited during those years. In the first of these, I stated (Phillips, 1965:2):

> In the social sciences today, the methods . . . have come increasingly to resemble those of the longer established "exact" sciences. The reliance on intuition, speculation, and more or less casual observation is diminishing and being replaced by research that accents the use of highly systematic, controlled procedures.

And in the second of these books I pointed out that (Phillips, 1967b: 3), "Using empirical methods, these . . . studies add considerably to our knowledge of human behavior and social processes in American society."

Let me now try to explain why these are no longer my views. First of all, I gradually became convinced that my own research did not really make a difference. About three years ago, I began to ask myself the question: Does my work really contribute anything to sociological knowledge? Up until that time I had considered the question only fleetingly, being rather certain that my work was not really in question as to its quality or importance. Similarly, I had assumed that if one's work had merit it would be published and that these published writings in some way would have an impact or influence on the field, i.e., added to the corpus of sociological knowledge. But in pondering this question, I became increasingly doubtful that this was the case. By that time, I had published some dozen or so articles—some of them in what are considered the better sociological journals. And I had profited from my publications; promotions and salary increases accompanied their appearance. While these rewards were a source of some satisfaction, they were not sufficient justification for the expenditure of time and money involved in my research activities. What I lacked was the feeling of accomplishment that comes from doing something of, even minor, importance. For, as I came to see it, my published work in no way "added up" with the results of other investigators to become part of the accumulation of sociological knowledge—correcting, extending, and refining what was previously known. This was especially distressing to me in that I had long ago acknowledged the failure of sociology to have any relevance for practical, real world concerns. Thus, I now came to believe that sociology not only fails to affect the world around us, but that, furthermore, sociology in no way represents some codified, cumulative body of knowledge.

This is not to say that my actual involvement in doing research was not a vast source of pleasure to me. For it was, and still is. Rather what disturbed me was the question: "So what?" Would it make any difference to anyone besides myself should I never publish anything further? Troubled by these questions, I began to ask other sociologists about their views on this matter. For it obviously occurred to me that the problem was perhaps my own, or one that young sociologists frequently encounter. After all, I had not published very much, my studies were small ones, I had not yet written a book, and my research interests were in areas of no particular concern to the great majority of sociologists. In raising these questions with other sociologists, I found that few seemed to understand the question of "So what?" with regard to one's work. This was generally true of young and old alike. And few took my questions very seriously. Usually the answers were of the quality: "You shouldn't feel that way, after all your work must be important or else it wouldn't have been published in ———" or "What do you mean by that question; your work is as important as most people's. Do you really think that what other people do (historians, businessmen, whatever) is really that important?" or "It takes a few years for one's work to become known, but then you'll see how much it contributes." Despite my insistent probing, including questions as to the contributions of their work, most of those whom I talked with seemed totally unwilling to pursue the "So what?" question. Rather, they all emphasized the importance of getting on with the task of doing sociology.

At the same time that this was occurring, there arose in the universities of the land a great fear that our graduate students would no longer be permitted draft-exempt status to complete their studies. A great hue and cry arose that this dangerous government action would result in a vast shortage of Ph.D.'s and that society would suffer for this ill-conceived policy. Given my doubts about sociology, I took this opportunity to quiz my colleagues and our graduate students as to exactly why this possible loss of Ph.D.-sociologists was such a disaster. Once again, their answers were of the quality: "Why ask me that? Our work is as important as that of historians, businessmen. . . ."

The second thing that led me to thoroughly question many of my earlier beliefs about sociology was the 1968 meetings of the American Sociological Association, where Martin Nicolaus, a member of the Sociology Liberation Movement, addressed some highly critical remarks to the assembled audience of sociologists. He described the sociological researcher as a "kind of spy," and observed (Nicolaus, 1969:155) that, "The more adventurous sociologists don the disguise of the people and go out to mix with the peasants in the 'field,' returning with the books and articles that break the protective secrecy in which a subjugated population wraps itself, and make it more accessible to manipulation and control." Nicolaus, then, was accusing sociologists of taking knowledge from the people and giving it to the rulers. Nicolaus (1969:155) went on to ask:

What if the machinery were reversed? What if the habits, problems, actions, and decisions of the wealthy and powerful were daily scrutinized by a thousand systematic researchers, were hourly pried into, analyzed, and cross-referenced, tabulated, and published in a hundred mass-circulated journals and written so that even the fifteen-year-old high school drop-out could understand it and predict the actions of their parents' landlord, manipulate and control *him*?

What surprised me about Nicolaus' remarks was not his assertion that sociologists are the servants of the power structure (for I generally shared that persuasion) but rather his apparent belief that sociologists actually know something that could be used *for* those in power and *against* what he calls the "occupied populace." I recognize that sociologists often lend legitimacy to the actions of the government and ruling class, but that a young radical sociologist should share with the sociological elite the belief that sociologists possess some unique knowledge that can be put to the use of one or another segment of the society was unexpected by me. Martin Nicolaus' remarks were, as I have indicated, another source of disquiet as far as my views of sociology were concerned.

Following the 1968 ASA meetings, I began to take a good hard look at the claims and actual accomplishments of sociology. There was, of course, no dearth of evidence on these matters, as many sociologists had long expressed highly critical views of the discipline. I was familiar with the writings of Mills and Gouldner, but for the first time I began to give careful attention to their criticisms. It became rather apparent to me that the model of value-free research was erroneous and inapplicable to much of sociology, that sociology contained few laws or general propositions that had empirical support, that sociologists focused on individuals and were seldom involved in the actual observation of behavior or interaction, and that the correspondence between people's *reports* to sociological investigators and their actual behavior is presently unknown. My overall conclusion was that individuals acquainted with certain sociological theories are unlikely to know any more about the real world than people who are unfamiliar with these theories. Despite all the claims that sociology is the "scientific study of human social behavior," it became clear to me that sociology, as actually practiced, falls far short of achieving this claim.

The third, and last, event that provided the impetus for the writing of this book came about from my concern with the adequacy of field studies of mental illness, a subject about which I had long been concerned. Since these studies are discussed at some length in Chapter II, I will take space here to mention only the events that are relevant to this book. During the fall of 1968, Kevin Clancy and I were very much involved in the analysis of data concerning the relationship between people's assessments as to the "social desirability" of mental health inventory items and their reports as to whether or not they had experienced the various symptoms constituting the inventory. In the process of writing up our findings, I turned to an examination of the literature not only on social desirability but also on bias, invalidity, error, artifacts, response sets and related issues. Reading the work of Crowne and Marlowe (1964), Rosenthal (1966), Edwards (1959), Friedman (1967), Nunnally

(1967), and others, I was overwhelmed by just how vast a literature existed in psychology with regard to problems of measurement in the collection of their data.

Although sociologists sometimes address these issues, there is nothing in sociology that is comparable to the very excellent studies by Friedman and Rosenthal. Psychologists seem to have been much more alert than sociologists to the relevance of ideas about "definitions of the situation" for empirical research. As sociologists, we all know that an individual's attitudes, opinions, and behavior are influenced by his perceptions of the interpersonal situations in which he finds himself. Despite the fact that we all *know* this, most sociologists seem unwilling to view the administration of an interview in a survey or the filling out of a self-administered questionnaire as forms of interaction—either real or symbolic. Sociologists, therefore, frequently fail to recognize the extent to which these "miniature social situations" (Hyman, 1949) may make our measuring instruments *less valid*. Psychologists, as I have indicated, are much more sensitive to these possibilities.

What becomes further apparent as one looks at books and articles on sociological methodology is that sociologists give heavy emphasis to problems of data-analysis but comparatively little attention to problems and strategies for data collection, which essentially involve questions of measurement. Although a few books, such as Cicourel's (1964) *Method and Measurement in Sociology* and Sjoberg and Nett's (1968) *A Methodology for Social Research,* do a good job of alerting sociologists to what are crucial measurement problems, there has been no systematic consideration of the sources and consequences of various factors operating in the process of data collection in sociology.

The impact of these materials on my own work and interests was considerable. One result was that I eventually abandoned a book on which I had been working for some months, in that I had acquired strong doubts about the validity of my data. A second result of having encountered these materials was that I began to search the literature of both sociology and psychology for information on the wide variety of factors that operate in data-collection activities (many of which are discussed in Chapters II and III). In pursuing this evidence, I became convinced of the need to bring these findings together in such a way that they would be readily available to other interested social scientists. I also became persuaded that our measurements of most variables were caused less by the "true" values of these variables than by the effects of measuring them. And I concluded that the processes operating in the collection of data about social phenomena are exactly the same processes which operate in many everyday social situations. Thus, I came to believe that by understanding what happens when the sociologist collects his data, we can better accomplish our goal of learning about everyday human behavior.

Having reached this conclusion, I began writing this book. In so doing, my initial concern was with improving the quality of sociological data—especially those data obtained through survey interviews. Or, as my colleague Alan Blum somewhat harshly put it to me, my interest was in finding ways to "repair the data." While writing the initial draft of the first few chapters, however, my concerns changed as I reexamined some of the methodological issues raised by the greatest of all sociologists: Max Weber. Reading Weber, I began to consider anew problems which I had largely ignored since my days as a graduate student. Paramount among these is the problem of how to understand the *meanings* of people's actions; i.e., what meanings individuals' actions have *for them*. Related to this is a second problem for sociological investigators: how to communicate the procedures for understanding to other sociologists. My attempts to grapple with these issues led me to reassess my thinking about what was necessary for the improvement of data-collection procedures in sociology, and to devote greater attention to trying to provide guidelines for getting at actors' meanings. The results of my endeavors in this regard constitute the bulk of Chapters VI and VII of this book.

In a sense, I suppose that I have at least temporarily answered my earlier "so what" question. For, at the present time, it seems to me that by paying closer attention to the methodological and theoretical issues involved in the actual carrying out of sociological research we may begin to widen the gap between what sociologists know and what everybody else knows. Hopefully, this book is a short step in that direction.

The present report, then, is my attempt to deal with some of these issues of data collection. As I have tried to indicate, it grew out of my doubts about the field of sociology—my feeling that we do not really know very much, and my perception that not many of my sociological brethren share my view—and my consequent receptivity to the writings of certain critics of the discipline and to the work of psychologists such as Friedman and Rosenthal, who were concerned with crucial methodological issues. Had I believed that sociologists were actually the scientists that many claim to be, in possession of much unique knowledge, I would probably have continued to ignore the critics and to view problems concerning the sources of our data as just minor sources of annoyance. Like most sociologists, I would have remained content to accept the rhetoric of the discipline and to imitate the surface features of the physical sciences.

In writing this book, my intention is threefold. First, the materials contained herein may help some sociological researchers in their own research activities, and will hopefully persuade all sociologists of the intimate interdependence of methodology and theory. Second, I wish to remind sociologists of the enormous complexity of social life—a complexity that is no less in the data-collection process than in other areas of social life. And, finally, I consider it important for the reader to become aware of exactly how little sociology has to say about the social world in which we live. This is especially important for protecting students from a vast amount of propaganda—propaganda that frequently has as its source the findings and "expert testimony" of members of the sociological profession. With regard to such findings, I fully endorse Chomsky's (1969:342) caution that "it will be quite unfortunate, and highly dangerous, if they are not accepted and judged on their merits and according to their actual, not pretended, accomplishments."

That, then, is how I came to do this book. But before moving on to consider its contents, something must be said about its title. Robert S. Lynd first published a book entitled *Knowledge for What?* in 1939 in which he chastised his fellow social scientists for their unwillingness to utilize their knowledge for the betterment of mankind. He argued that in many instances social scientists already possessed the knowledge necessary for bringing about certain societal benefits; he asserted (Lynd, 1964:241), for instance, that "the causes of war are known and accepted by a wide group of thoughtful students." Lynd felt that there were other areas of social concern where social scientists had a special expertise.

Obviously, I do not share Lynd's views. For I see no corpus of sociological knowledge, or at least I find no corpus of knowledge that is *unique* to sociology. The fact that we still lack such knowledge is bothersome enough, but even more troublesome is our inability to recognize that this is the case. Clearly there is much that passes for knowledge in the rhetoric of the social sciences. Much of this so-called knowledge is used by privileged elites to provide a facade of rationality for their actions. And much of it is fed to them by the kingpins of our discipline, those whom Nicolaus terms "intellectual valets" and "secular priests." We should begin to acknowledge that, like ourselves, there is much they do not know. As intellectuals, we must not surrender our role as dispassionate critics. We must insist upon the truth, whenever and wherever the truth can be known. Hence, while I wish I could seriously entertain Lynd's question of "Knowledge for What?," the more appropriate question, to my mind, is the one posed in the title of this book: "Knowledge from What?"

Chapter I

Sources and Limitations of Sociological Data

Over the past seventy-five years or so, millions of dollars have been spent on empirical investigations of various social phenomena, including crime, delinquency, racial conflict, status striving, religious behavior, marriage and divorce, voting, physical and mental illness, sexual practices, births and deaths, and a wide variety of other behaviors. Thousands of technical reports have appeared in various sociological journals, and dozens of textbooks and research monographs have been published annually. Taken together, these technical reports, research monographs, and textbooks constitute the corpus of sociological knowledge. This knowledge is transmitted to college students and others in ever-increasing numbers as the population grows and as sociology becomes more and more popular and more respectable as a field of study. It seems clear that sociology has come to occupy a secure position in American colleges and universities, and that it is seen as capable of making significant contributions in other sectors of the society as well (see Lazarsfeld et al., *The Uses of Sociology,* 1967). In fact, sociologists have increasingly gained access to the corridors of power in American society.

Given that sociology has "arrived" and that its knowledge of social phenomena is deemed important and useful by students and politicians alike, it seems reasonable to ask some questions about the state of sociology as it is practiced today. Let us begin by inquiring about the *sources* of sociological knowledge. Where does our knowledge come from? What are the means by which sociologists gather the information (the data) which constitutes the accumulated knowledge of the discipline? A second question concerns the matter of *how much* we know. Do we have empirical generalizations that adequately explain the social phenomena with which we are concerned?

Consider, first, the sources of sociological knowledge. All social science data are obtained in either formal or informal settings and involve either verbal (oral and written) or nonverbal acts or responses (Galtung, 1967:110). Various combinations of the two settings for data collection and the two types of manifest responses give rise to the several major techniques which sociologists employ in collecting their empirical data: observation of behavior, experiments, reports by others, analyses of existing records and documents, interviews, and questionnaires. At the one extreme where the focus is on nonverbal actions in informal settings, participant observation is the most common data-collection procedure. At the other extreme where the emphasis is on verbal (oral and written) acts in formal, structured settings, the most common modes of data collection are precoded interviews and structured questionnaires (Galtung, 1967:110).

One might suppose that the principal research techniques would involve the observation of behavior, in that behavior is the main focus of most sociological investigations. However, this is not usually the case. As Coleman (1969:109) notes: ". . . most research techniques which analyze behavioral data take a short cut in data collection, and base their methods on individuals' reports of their own behavior and less frequently, on those of others." And Webb and his associates (1966) point out that the dominant mass of social science today is based upon interviews and questionnaires, and this is especially the case with sociology.[1]

[1] Later on in this report, consideration will be given to *why* there should be such a

A rough idea of just how dominant these two data-collection procedures are in sociology can be seen from the results of my examination of all articles and research notes published in the *American Sociological Review,* the official journal of the American Sociological Association, for the years 1962–1969. This examination revealed that approximately 90 per cent of the articles and research notes presenting analyses of empirical data are based on data collected by way of interviews and questionnaires. The remaining 10 per cent are based on other data-collection procedures: historical documents, available records, content analyses of various materials, experiments, and direct and indirect observations.[2] Brown and Gilmartin (1969) reached a similar conclusion in their examination of research articles published in the *American Sociological Review* and the *American Journal of Sociology* during 1965–1966. They found that 91.7 per cent of the research articles based on primary data had utilized interviews and/or questionnaires. The authors (Brown and Gilmartin, 1969:288) state that: "Six inquiries were based on participant observation, but in almost every instance the investigators felt compelled to add supplementary facts from structured interviews to bolster their conclusions. Other anthropological techniques were completely ignored. Life histories and personal documents were seldom gathered."

Thus, most of our scientific conclusions and generalizations about social behavior and interaction are based on materials secured by asking individuals to reveal—either in their own words or through acceptance or rejection of standardized items—their feelings, beliefs, attitudes, and experiences regarding some issue, idea, behavior, or other area of interest to the investigator.

Frequently in these interview and questionnaire studies, the

---

heavy emphasis and reliance on the use of questionnaires and interviews in sociological research. Attention will also be given to some of the advantages and disadvantages of alternative data-collection procedures.

[2] Obviously, I do not know whether this small representation of studies based on techniques other than interviews and questionnaires reflects: (1) the actual research techniques used by sociologists, (2) the techniques used by sociological researchers who submit articles for consideration by the ASR, or (3) the standards of the journal's editors. Undoubtedly, all of these factors, and others as well, play a part in determining the content of this journal. The point to be made, however, is that the vast majority of sociological studies is based on data obtained from interviews and questionnaires.

individual is asked to reveal his behavior or feelings in the near or distant past. How often did he visit with friends last week? Whom did he vote for last year? Did he enjoy school when he was nine years old? Sometimes he is asked to imagine how he might act in some future situation or circumstance. Would he move if a Negro moved in next door? Would he vote for a woman for President? But probably most often the individual is asked to supply something more in the nature of a self-report concerning his present status. Usually this involves a series of statements which a person is asked to rate as being applicable or descriptive of himself ("true for you") or inapplicable or undescriptive of himself ("not true for you"). For example, people are asked to respond to the following types of statements: "I have personal worries that get me down physically." "Most people should be expected to handle their own problems." "When it comes right down to it, you have to rely on yourself." And frequently in sociological research people are asked to provide what is ordinarily considered background information of a factual nature: age, sex, education level, occupation, income, marital status, religious affiliation, nationality, and the like.

It is often the case that sociologists are not concerned with people's responses per se but rather in the extent to which the responses are indicative of some past or future actions. Even in studies of attitudes, the researcher is frequently interested in how people behave in one or another circumstance. Usually, of course, this involves certain inferences in which the data are linked, in a causal chain, to the behavior of actual interest to the investigator. So, for instance, if one obtains data concerning people's attitudes toward various types of people (Negroes, Jews, the mentally ill), the assumption is frequently made that if similar persons were encountered in real life, the respondents would behave toward them in a manner consistent with their attitudes in the data-collection situation. Or, to provide a nonattitudinal example, if people endorse certain statements thought to be indicative of authoritarianism, the inference is made that they indeed possess authoritarian personalities and would behave in certain specified ways thought to be characteristic of persons with authoritarian personalities.

In both of the above examples, certain inferences are required of the researcher. As Sechrest (1968:530) notes, "Other things being equal we may take it as being certain that the more steps there are in an inferential process, the greater the probability of error." It also seems to be the case that inferences about nonverbal behavior which are based on verbal responses are more subject to distortion and error than are inferences about future or past nonverbal behavior which are based on the observation of such behavior. That is, it is easier to "lie with words" than to "lie with acts." More will be said about this particular point in a later chapter.

Galtung (1967:112), however, has argued that verbal responses are always of interest, in that they serve as a basis for the inference of future verbal behavior. Yet, most sociologists profess to be more interested in *social interaction* than in future verbal behavior. My own examination of twenty-one introductory sociology textbooks reveals that fifteen define sociology as the study (or science) of interaction, human relationships, human behavior, or social processes. Two emphasize terms other than the above in their definitions, while four books provide no formal definitions of sociology at all. Most of these introductory textbooks give as their focus, then, a concern with the behavior of individuals (and groups of individuals) in social interaction with one another.

A large segment of the studies which these authors cite as providing for various generalizations about behavior and interaction are based on data collected through questionnaires and interviews. Unfortunately, these two modes of data collection do not really provide direct access to either behavior or social interaction—although the results obtained with these two data-collection procedures are often discussed *as if* they had been investigated. This is true as well for most of the sociological propositions contained in the Berelson and Steiner (1964) book, *Human Behavior: An Inventory of Scientific Findings*. In short, despite the wide variety of data-collection techniques available to the sociologist, the most frequently employed procedures do not directly observe either individuals' behavior or their interactions with others. Brown and Gilmartin (1969:288) have remarked on this too, saying that:

It would seem that our colleagues tend to ignore actual behavioral patterns and also fail to come to grips with the fundamental problem of the relation of attitudes and sentiments to behavior. To an even greater extent, sociology is becoming the study of verbally expressed sentiments and feelings, rather than an analysis of human performance.

We find, then, that the *source* of much sociological knowledge is people's reports of their nonverbal behavior. Let us consider now the second question with which we began. How much do we know? Or, perhaps more properly, how well have sociologists done in realizing their specific purposes? This is a difficult question to answer in that there is no firm consensus among sociologists as to the purposes of sociological inquiry. However, there does seem to be general agreement among sociologists that the principal purpose of sociological research is to establish generalizations showing relationships of dependence between stated social phenomena. It is widely acknowledged that all such generalizations in the discipline of sociology are statistical or probabilistic, in that they do not occur invariably or with strict universality. This means that if it is asserted, for instance, that "there is an inverse relationship between social class and mental illness," this is not meant to suggest that all lower class persons and no upper class persons are mentally ill. Nor is this intended to mean that an inverse relationship is maintained in all places at all times. What is intended by such an assertion, however, is that there is a correlation between social class and mental health status that is inverse in character. Additionally, of course, this correlation in some way should *make sense* theoretically to the investigator and other sociologists.

Given this goal of establishing empirical generalizations about theoretically relevant social phenomena, we still must consider the adequacy of such generalizations. Here, the dominant emphasis in sociology is on the importance of *explanation* and *prediction*. The view of Smelser is probably rather typical of those who hold this view. He asserts that (Smelser, 1969:13–14): "Explanation...begins with the search for *independent variables* (or causes, or determinants, or factors, or conditions), to which variations in the dependent variables are referred." He goes on to offer the principle (Smelser, 1969:19) that "no investigative activity in sociology is scientifically legitimate unless it can be related directly to the core sociological enterprise: accounting for variations and interdependencies of data within a sociological framework." And Coleman (1969:107) states that "one of the important fruits of sociological investigation should be its ability to predict."

This concern with explanation and prediction dominates contemporary American sociology. However, there are some sociologists who choose to evaluate the success or failure of their research endeavors in terms of "understanding." Those holding this viewpoint are a minority among sociologists, and I will postpone discussion of their views until a later chapter.

For now, let us ask whether sociologists in the positivistic tradition—those emphasizing explanation and prediction have realized their purposes Have they achieved their goals? I think that the answer to this is clearly "no." For despite the vast expenditure of money, and of time and manpower as well, sociologists have been generally unable to provide generalizations that explain very much of the social behavior in which they are interested. While there are indeed literally dozens, if not hundreds, of generalizations abounding in the sociological literature, the vast majority are either unconfirmed in empirical research or else are of such minor magnitude in explaining any observable facts as to be of limited utility. Regarding such generalizations or propositions, Whyte (1969b:22) relates that "years ago the late Louis Wirth used to terrify Ph.D. candidates by requiring them to name *one* proposition that had been reasonably well supported by research data." In my view, contemporary sociologists would be as hard pressed as the students of Wirth's era in naming one such proposition.

One way of considering this problem is in terms of the amount of variance in their dependent variables which sociologists are able to account for by their principal independent variables. The sociologists' aim, of course, is to find a relatively small number of basic variables that will explain the variation in many other variables.[3] The variance in one variable is said to be explained by

[3] It would also be useful to develop a relatively small number of measures of such variables, thus allowing for greater concern with their validity and for the replication of studies in which the same measures are employed. At the present time, there are almost as many different measures utilized by sociologists as there are studies of social phenomena. Some indication of this can be seen from the results obtained by Bonjean et al. (1967) who—in examining every article and research note over a twelve-year period (1954–1965) in the *American Journal of Sociology,*

another to the extent that the variables covary or correlate. Thus if mental health status correlates highly with social class position, mental health status is, at one level or another, explained by social class position. However, examination of the extent to which certain sociological variables are able to explain the variation in other variables is rather unimpressive. For example, Hamblin (1966) cites a paper by L. K. Miller in which he examined the results of articles published in the first three issues of the *American Sociological Review* in the year 1961, and found that the average "significant" relationship explained about 10 per cent of the variance. And the psychologist Robert Rosenthal (1966:110) estimates that most behavioral research can account for something like 13 per cent of the variance by our independent variables. Clearly, an ability to account for only 10 or 13 or even 20 per cent of the variance is not very impressive, and does not lead to a high degree of predictive ability.[4] However, this problem is largely ignored by sociologists, and there is very little in the sociological literature that faces up to the inability of our independent variables to explain much variance in the dependent variables of empirical interest. One sociologist who has remarked on this shortcoming is Alvin Gouldner (1959:248) who observes:

the *American Sociological Review, Social Forces,* and *Sociometry*—found that (Bonjean et al., 1967:9–10): "there were 3,609 attempts to measure various phenomena by the use of scales or indices and 2,080 different measures were used. Of the measures used, only 589 (28.3 per cent of the total number of scales and indices) were used more than once. . . . The lack of continuity in social research is reflected further by the observation that of the 2,080 scales and indices appearing in the journals over the twelve-year period covered by the analysis, only 47, or 2.26 per cent, were used more than five times." For instance, eighteen different scales and indices were used in twenty-one different studies of "cohesion." Forty-seven measures of crime and delinquency were used in sixty-four different studies.

[4] The main exception to this would appear to be demographical and ecological studies where the emphasis is on explaining regularities and variations in births and deaths, population size, and physical movements. One reason why these two fields (and demography especially) have been able to explain a larger proportion of the variance than have other research concerns is that the independent and dependent variables of chief interest are rather easily identified and measured. Most people are in agreement as to what constitutes a birth or a death, and the variables to which they are frequently related, such as age, sexual status, and race. But even here, there are difficulties in accounting for the associations between some of the variables. That is, when investigators attempt to utilize various social-psychological and sociocultural variables in explaining certain empirical consistencies, they frequently offer generalizations with an extremely low degree of explanatory power.

There is a fairly widespread tendency among sociologists to rest content with a demonstration that some sociological variable "makes a difference." If a variable can be shown to control even the smallest proportion of the variance in a problematic matter, it is all too readily regarded as a memorable contribution to sociology and all too ceremoniously ushered into its theoretical hall of fame. . . . Unless sustained interest is manifested in the degree of variance which a variable controls, and, unless, further, we can identify sociological variables that certifiably control substantial proportions of the variance in the specified patterns of human behavior, sociology will remain scientifically immature and practically ineffectual.

Hamblin (1966:3), too, has commented on the general lack of concern among sociologists for the degree of explained variance: "there appears to be a gentlemen's agreement among readers and editors never to demand measures of explained variance, usually just significance tests. Why? In part, perhaps, because the measures of explained variance are so embarrassing to all."

Whatever the reasons may be for a lack of demand for measures of explained variance, it seems appropriate that we consider another question. Why is it that those sociologists concerned with explanation and prediction are unable to account for more than a small portion of the variance in their research? Considering this question, Blalock (1968:157) has offered three possibilities: (1) researchers may be dealing with the wrong set of independent variables; (2) there may be a large number of independent variables operating more or less simultaneously; and (3) sociologists may be studying the right variables, but the unexplained variance is perhaps due to inadequate measurement.

In my view, however, Blalock ignores another possibility in his consideration of problems of unexplained variance: the effects of the *data-collection procedures* themselves on the properties being measured. It is a guiding thesis of this book that *the variables which arise from the data-collection activity itself are a major source of influence on the behavior and responses (i.e., variance) of subjects in sociological investigations.* That is, it is argued that data collection is a social process, sharing features in common with other social situations and events of human interaction. What this means is that even though sociologists seldom *observe* behavior (in that they rely heavily on questionnaires and interviews), there *is* behavior involved in most sociological investigations: that behavior which constitutes the data-collection process itself. In other words, much of our knowledge of social behavior results from the behavior involved in the process of collecting data.

Now the above thesis is not novel to me. Other critics of present-day sociological research have also laid heavy stress on the social nature of the data-collection process (e.g., Cicourel, 1964; Denzin, 1970; Sjoberg and Nett, 1968). Where this report differs from others is in the attempt to accomplish several different goals: (1) to consider the above view in light of a considerable amount of *empirical* evidence regarding the present shortcomings of much sociological research, (2) to examine this view with regard to some of the processes operating in ordinary social interaction, and (3) to suggest some alternate direction in the collection of sociological data.

Unfortunately, to achieve goals (1) and (2) above, it is necessary to draw upon the very sources of sociological knowledge that I have just raised questions about. This becomes especially apparent in the chapter that follows, where I cite a number of studies concerning bias in social science research. These studies where bias is considered may, of course, themselves have been subject to biasing influences. In fact, we can imagine the existence of systematic bias in a study that was designed to uncover systematic bias in a study that was designed to uncover systematic bias in a study that was . . . ad infinitum. I am afraid that the air of paradox created by my citations of empirical studies which support my thesis is ultimately unavoidable. But I would hope that recognition of this problem—and the doubts it may raise in the reader's mind—will tend to underscore my arguments concerning the social nature of data collection and the trustworthiness of our data. With Rosenberg (1969:14), I share the view that "there is nothing more restorative of the scientific temper than an occasional encounter with the hard, intractable fact that one has made, and remains capable of making, mistakes."

To summarize, in this brief chapter I have reached three conclusions with regard to contemporary sociology: first, that most sociological knowledge is based ultimately on people's *reports* of their behavior, rather than on the actual observation of behavior and interaction; second, that with regard to *how much* we know, the ability of most sociological researchers to explain or predict relationships between social phenomena is very limited; and third, that one reason why explanation and prediction are of such a low magnitude is that sociologists tend to underestimate the influence of their data-collection procedures on the phenomena which they attempt to measure. Later on in this report, I will argue that there is an overdependence on interviews and questionnaires and that they are frequently (perhaps usually) utilized in inappropriate circumstances. In the chapter that follows, however, I will consider measurement problems in sociology—mainly as they pertain to data obtained from survey interviews. My intention is to show that questions of validity are paramount in sociological investigations and that biases and measurement errors are characteristic of much sociological research. I will argue that these biases and errors are an almost necessary consequence of the data-collection procedures most heavily utilized by social scientists. While from one point of view, many of the factors arising in the collection of sociological data can be seen as biases, from another perspective they represent the *very essence* of human interaction and communication. Thus, the third chapter considers these biasing factors not as biases per se but rather as elements common to ordinary social interaction. Then in Chapter IV, I suggest how these elements of everyday behavior may operate in the most common type of data-collection procedure in sociology: survey research. Chapter V focuses on the use and improvement of the interview in survey studies. In Chapter VI I discuss two alternative methods for collecting sociological data: unobtrusive measures and observational techniques. Finally, in Chapter VII, I devote my attention to methodological issues concerning studies designed to get at the meaning of social actions. Central to that presentation is a concern with the importance of personal involvement and personal experience in the study of various social phenomena.

Chapter II

Invalidity and Bias in Social Research: An Examination of the Literature

Since it is my view that the data-collection process often has an unrecognized influence on the results of sociological investigations, it is useful to consider this influence in terms of difficulties in measurement. Measurement is, of course, the *sine qua non* of any science. If the validity of any theoretical statement is to be evaluated, it is necessary to obtain measures of all the variables contained in that statement. And for theories to stand on empirical observations, valid and reliable observations must be gathered. Thus, problems of measurement constitute a key to the advancement of sociology. In a broad sense, most of the content of this book is concerned with problems of measurement in sociology. Let us turn, then, to a consideration of some of these measurement problems.

MEASUREMENT PROBLEMS IN SOCIOLOGY

Recently, both Blalock and Hauser have remarked on the significance of measurement problems to sociological research Blalock

(1969a:115) observes that 'certain kinds of inadequacies in our measurement procedures may very well provide the major obstacle to be overcome if sociology is to mature in the direction of becoming a 'hard' and disciplined social science." And Hauser (1969) asserts that the problem of adequate measurement is the major block to progress in sociological research. He goes on to say (Hauser, 1969:127–128):

> I should like to venture the judgment that it is inadequate measurement, more than inadequate concept or hypothesis, that has plagued social researchers and prevented fuller explanations of the variances with which they are confounded. The problem of obtaining precise enough measurements of the items with which we work and of avoiding confounded variables has probably retarded sociology more than the absence of more powerful analytical procedures.

One way of viewing these measurement problems is to point out that, whenever social scientists collect data, differences among individuals on various measures can arise from a wide variety of factors. Some of these differences (variations) may be thought of as being due to true differences among people in the attributes, qualities, characteristics, or whatever, that are being measured. However, some of these differences represent errors in measurement. The major problem in evaluating the results of any measurement procedure is that of determining what shall be considered as true differences in whatever it is the investigator is attempting to measure and what shall be considered as variations due to errors in measurement. In discussing this problem, Selltiz et al. (1959:150–154) list several possible sources of difference among individuals on various measures: (1) true differences in the characteristic which one is attempting to measure, (2) true differences in other relatively stable characteristics of the individual which affect his score, (3) differences due to transient personal factors, (4) differences arising from situational factors, (5) differences because of variations in administration, (6) differences due to sampling of items, (7) differences resulting from an instrument's lack of clarity, (8) differences due to mechanical factors, and (9) differences arising from factors in the analysis of the data.

Ideally, of course, all of the differences among people on various measures would be due entirely to true differences in whatever it is the investigator is attempting to measure. Thus, if we were measuring mental health status, all of the differences among individuals' scores on a mental health inventory (or whatever measures of mental health were being employed) would be due to actual differences in their mental health status Or, if the concern were with differences in people's religiosity, the differences among people on a measure of religiosity would represent true differences in their religiosity. In both examples. none of the differences would, ideally. reflect chance variation or the effects of other variables.

While the ideal is that differences among people on various measures reflect true differences, the reality is that no measurement is entirely free from error. Still, the goal of scientists is to reduce errors to a minimum. These measurement errors are of two types: constant and random errors. *Constant* (or biasing) errors are introduced into the measurement by some factor that systematically (in one direction or another) affects either that which is being measured or the process of measurement. *Random* errors, on the other hand, arise from those transient aspects of the individual, the measurement procedure, the situation of measurement, etc., that are apt to vary from one measurement to the next, even though that which is being measured has not changed. Both random and constant errors affect estimates of *validity*, while *reliability* is usually affected only by random errors.

Several of the factors listed above as contributing to variations among measurement results may lead to constant or systematic errors. It is these variations involved in the data-collection process itself, thereby affecting our measurement procedures and resulting in a systematic bias, that will constitute a major concern of this report. Hence, my focus is on questions of validity rather than reliability. Any scientist is, of course, concerned that his measures be both reliable and valid. For that reason, brief mention will be made of the matter of reliability. *Reliability* refers to the extent to which a measuring instrument is likely to yield a consistent score or result (Green, 1954). Selltiz et al. (1959:148) define reliability as follows: "independent but comparable measures of the same object (or attitude, or whatever) should give similar results (provided, of course, that there is no reason to believe that the object being measured has in fact changed between the two measurements)." This is distinctly different from the question of validity; for we may have totally reliable information about an individual that is absolutely invalid for whatever purpose it was intended. We might, for instance, have very reliable information as to people's educational accomplishments, but this may or may not be a valid indicator of how well they will perform on a certain job. Or a reliable measure might be obtained as to how often people are bothered by nervousness or headaches, but these may not be valid measures of their mental health status.

More important than reliability, however, is *validity*—which represents the key concept for considering the adequacy of measurement. Generally the matter of the validity of a measure concerns the question as to whether it, in fact, measures what it purports to measure (Cannell and Kahn, 1968). The problem—and it is one of the major methodological problems of the social sciences —is just *how it may be determined that an instrument measures what it purports to measure.* Obviously, we do not usually know an individual's true location on the variable we are attempting to measure. Hence, there is no direct way of determining the validity of the measure. If his true location were known, there would, of course, be no need for our measure—unless the measure were easier, less expensive, or more appropriate to administer. This means that the validity of a measuring instrument must be judged in terms of the extent to which its results are deemed comparable with other relevant evidence. And what constitutes relevant evidence for one investigator may not be regarded as such by another.

While questions of validity and reliability are discussed in all methodology textbooks in sociology, they are seldom given much attention in the actual research activities and reports of sociological researchers.[1] Reliability is occasionally mentioned in reports of empirical investigations. Questions of validity are almost com-

[1] A notable, and important, exception to this is the work of the psychologist Charles Cannell and his associates at the Survey Research Center, University of Michigan. For several years they have been involved in research to determine some of the variables affecting the accuracy of health information collected by personal interviews and self-enumerative procedures. See, for example, Cannell and Fowler (1963, 1964) and Cannell et al. (1968).

pletely ignored. Estimates of reliability and validity are both of great importance to any empirical undertaking, but the latter is by far the more important of the two. For it is possible, as mentioned earlier, to have a highly reliable instrument that is totally invalid. But if we have a valid measure, it must, of necessity, be reliable to some degree. Yet, as Selltiz et al. (1959:277) have noted, "many—probably most—questionnaires and interviews have been used without evidence of their validity."

One reason why so many sociologists have chosen to ignore the question of validity may be because it is such a difficult concept to come to grips with. Here it is useful to quote Sechrest (1968:559) who states the matter quite clearly:

> Exactly what is meant by the validity of a test [or any other instrument] is often quite unclear. Strictly speaking, of course, a test is valid as a predictor for anything with which it correlates. Such a conception of validity has been termed *empirical* validity by Anastasi and viewed in such a way the validity of a measure can be expressed precisely by a correlation coefficient. However, it becomes quite evident that, if validity is approached in a strictly empirical manner, there is no such thing as *the* validity of a test. As Guilford and Loevinger have pointed out, a test has as many "validity" coefficients as there are things with which it might be correlated.

An important task, then, is to determine what would be relevant or appropriate criteria for determining the validity of a measuring instrument. Let us consider this problem by examining the types of validation procedures employed by social scientists.

With some measuring instruments, validity depends primarily on the adequacy with which some specified domain of content is sampled. An example of this would be a final examination for a course in sociology. Since the intent of the examination is not to predict something else but to directly measure performance with regard to some unit of instruction, the examination cannot be validated in terms of some outside criteria. In the case of *content* validity, as this type of validation is called, validation consists essentially in the making of a judgment as to the representativeness of the examination questions constituting the measure. An obvious problem here is that of determining what constitutes representative items or questions for there are no exact specifications for the determination of content validity.

A second type of validity, which is actually one aspect of content validity, is *face* validity. Here one merely considers the extent to which an instrument seems to measure what it is supposed to measure. Usually face validity concerns judgments about an instrument after it is constructed. The problem with face validity is that a measure which appears to be high in face validity may or may not be valid and since no exact operations for determining face validity have ever been specified, the utilization of measures which the investigator feels possess face validity are not likely to lead to valid generalizations in sociology. For if an item or an instrument may appear to one investigator to provide a high degree of face validity, it may appear to his critics as "on the face of it" totally lacking in validity. While in the field of psychology face validity has fallen into general disrepute, it is still the sole justification for the use of numerous measures by sociologists.

A third type of validity, and one which is seldom of concern to sociologists, is *pragmatic* validity of which there are two subtypes. The first is *concurrent* validity which refers to the extent to which a measure distinguishes individuals who differ in their present status on some measure of interest to the investigator. The second, *predictive* validity, refers to the adequacy of a measure in distinguishing persons who will differ with respect to some future criteria. So, for instance, the concurrent validity of a mental health inventory might be examined in terms of its ability to distinguish between "well" persons and those currently under psychiatric care. Similarly, a mental health inventory's predictive validity might consist of correlating scores on the inventory with actual psychiatric care at some future time. Frequently, of course, the criteria against which an instrument's pragmatic validity is compared may themselves be of doubtful validity. With some matters of interest to social researchers, however, there are generally agreed upon criteria against which to validate a measure's pragmatic validity. Items asking people's age or marital status would have high pragmatic validity if a strong correlation between their item responses and their true age and marital status (as revealed by birth certificates and marriage records) were to be found. Although, as will be emphasized at several points in this report, many items commonly included within the sociologist's research instruments could be similarly validated, very seldom is there an actual attempt to do so.

The type of validity of most explicit concern to sociologists is *construct* validity which is usually involved in situations where the researcher has no definite criterion measure of the attribute, characteristic, quality, or whatever with which he is concerned and must use indirect measures. To the extent that a variable, say social class, is abstract rather than concrete, it can be spoken of as a construct. Here the attribute or quality underlying the measure is of central importance, rather than either people's scores on an instrument or scores on the criterion. In part, the definition of such constructs consists of sets of propositions about their relationship to other variables of theoretical and empirical interest. As Selltiz puts it (Selltiz et al., 1959:159):

> Thus, in examining construct validity, it is appropriate to ask such questions as: What predictions would one make, on the basis of these sets of propositions, about the relationships to other variables of scores based on a measure of this construct? Are the measures obtained by using this instrument consistent with these predictions?

What this means, then, is that instead of worrying about whether individuals who are classified on the basis of their responses as "upper middle class," for example, are *really* upper middle class, one asks whether classifying them in this way, when put together with measures of other variables, yields predictive and explanatory control over the phenomena under study. If it does, and if it does so in a way that corresponds to the pattern that was hypothesized on the basis of regarding that measure as an indicator of class, then—the argument goes—one would be satisfied with the construct validity of that measure of social class (Menzel, 1968).

There is another method of validation which is, as far as can be determined, almost never considered by the sociological researcher. This is the *convergent-discriminant* conception of validity advanced by Campbell and Fiske (1959).[2] The notion of convergent validity is similar to that of construct validation, and involves the question of whether responses on a measure do or do not relate to some other variable or variables that one would, on *a priori* or theoretical grounds, expect it to relate to. While sociologists are concerned with construct or convergent validity, i.e., what an instrument purports to measure, they are largely unconcerned with establishing the ability of an instrument to distinguish one variable measured from another, i.e., its *discriminant* validity. As Sechrest (1968:561) emphasizes, "measures may be invalidated not only by showing that they correlate poorly with some criterion but also by showing that they correlate highly with some conceptually simpler variable, such as the tendency to respond true, or in a socially desirable manner to all items."

If it is shown that a measure is strongly related to certain other characteristics of the individual (such as intelligence) or of the situation (such as the desire to please the investigator), then the discriminant validity of the measure is impaired and its usefulness is open to question. To secure evidence of a measure's discriminant validity the investigator must also measure the characteristics or variables from which he wishes to differentiate his construct, using as much as possible the same general methods that he has used to measure his central construct. Imagine that a researcher was interested in studying "anti-Semitism." Prior to the actual utilization of his measure of anti-Semitism in his planned study, he might choose to determine the measure's ability to distinguish people's anti-Semitic attitudes from those toward people in general. If there turned out to be a high positive correlation between people's attitudes toward Jews and people in general, this would indicate that the anti-Semitism measure was unable to discriminate between specific attitudes toward Jews and a more general attitude toward mankind. In this case, the measure's discriminant validity would be called into question.

[2] Also important to Campbell and Fiske (1959), although it shall not concern us here, is the importance of gathering evidence to show that *different* measures of a construct yield similar results.

In the above discussion, several types of validity have been considered: face, pragmatic, construct, and convergent-discriminant validity. Whereas with content and face validity there are no empirical procedures for the validation of our measures, with the other types of validity we have seen that measures may be invalidated by showing that they correlate poorly with some outside criteria or that they correlate highly with some conceptually simpler variable. Measures may also be partially invalidated by other influences entering into the measurement procedure. As will be seen in the following pages, a measure's validity may be affected by such factors as interviewer characteristics and situational influences.

My intention in the remainder of this chapter is to review some of the social science literature pertaining to bias and invalidity in studies of various social phenomena. Our review begins with a brief discussion of several studies in which measures have been validated against outside criteria. Then, in the bulk of the chapter, my interest is in reviewing a great variety of studies involving bias and invalidity arising from the data-collection activity itself.

As I pointed out in Chapter I, the studies which I cite may themselves be subject to bias and invalidity. There is, unfortunately, no way of knowing whether or not this is the case. But let me remind the reader that my purpose in discussing studies of bias is to underscore the fact that biases exist in almost all sociological investigations. Hence, if the evidence cited suggests to the reader that the studies discussed herein are themselves subject to bias, I will have been at least partially successful in my quest to convince him of the problematic nature of much sociological knowledge. There is, I must acknowledge, a further shortcoming in the investigations cited in documenting the existence of bias and invalidity in social science research: these investigations have generally failed to provide estimates of either explained variance or the magnitude of different biasing factors. Nor have they, by and large, considered these biasing factors in combination but rather one at a time. Thus, it is impossible to determine exactly how much influence these biases have. But by examining a wide number of studies where bias has been discovered, it is my hope that even the most skeptical of readers will be convinced that elements in the data-collection process may be a major source of influence on the responses of individuals in social science investigations. Commenting on one aspect of this problem, response-errors, Hauser (1969:127) states:

> I am astonished by the failure of the studies of response-error in censuses and surveys to evoke more responses from sociologists and other social scientists. . . . I believe that it is at least a moot question as to whether, up to this point in the history of the use of survey results, more misinformation than information has been gathered on many subjects

As Hauser notes for response errors, most sociological investigators have tended to ignore the importance of the investigator's influence upon the results which he obtains.

I recognize, of course, that the biasing effects of some factors may work to counteract the biasing effects of others. But it is at least equally possible that the effects of these biases may be cumulative. In my view, the obligation for demonstrating that these elements within the data-collection process have no appreciable effects on the results of sociological research lies with the individual investigator. Hopefully, my enumeration of some of these elements will alert the sociological researcher to the need for more sophisticated research designs, as well as to the importance of considering alternate procedures for collecting his data. These two matters will be considered at length in Chapters V, VI, and VII. The point to be emphasized here is that a discipline which fails so miserably in achieving its announced purposes of explanation and prediction cannot afford to ignore the very factors that may play a part in bringing about that state of affairs. Let us begin, then, by examining the results of several studies where the validity of an instrument has been checked against some outside criterion.

VALIDATION AGAINST OUTSIDE CRITERIA

Much sociological research involves asking people to provide certain kinds of facts about themselves (their age, educational attainments, religious affiliation, marital status, occupations). These data frequently constitute the major variables in sociological studies. While it is usually possible to validate questionnaire and interview items of this nature against outside criteria, for the most part this is not done. People's responses are simply accepted as valid. In addition to obtaining this kind of information, questions are often directed at ascertaining whether people have engaged in certain kinds of activities: voting, criminal and delinquent activities, sexual practices, and so on. These, too, can sometimes be validated, although it is usually more difficult, expensive, and time-consuming. Still other investigations are concerned with people's attitudes about various matters, some as indicators of how people will behave at some future time or have acted in the past. The problem of validation here is somewhat different than with the above types of measures. It is clearly difficult to validate attitudinal measures, but the relationship between attitudes and actual behavior can sometimes be established. We shall now examine some of the evidence concerning these matters.

Turning first to investigations of voting and voting registration, Bell and Buchanan (1966) found that 30 per cent of the respondents in a general population gave inaccurate replies to a question on voting. Similar figures were obtained by Parry and Crossley (1950) who found that 23 per cent of their respondents said they had voted in a 1944 election when they actually had not done so, and by Cahalan (1968) who reports that 28 per cent of the respondents in Denver exaggerated their vote in the 1947 mayoralty election. Clausen (1968) examined the validity of people's responses on election day turnout and, based on a check of official records, estimated an invalidity rate of 6.9 per cent in the respondents' reports of their turnout on election day. And a study by Carol Weiss (1968) concerned with the validity of welfare mothers' interview responses found that (C. Weiss, 1968:624): "On the voting and registration questions, 82 per cent of the welfare mothers answered accurately. Sixteen per cent overreported their registration and 2 per cent underreported. The amount and direction of response error are similar to those of the largely middle-class populations whose voting self-reports have been validated in previous studies." Although the amount of inaccuracy differs in these studies, it seems clear that people's verbal reports are often, to varying degrees, not valid indicators of their actual voting behavior.

Another area where sociological knowledge is based on people's reports of their behavior is that concerning birth control information and usage. Numerous surveys have been conducted to ascertain the use of various contraceptive devices. People's responses to inquiries about the use of these devices have generally been assumed to be valid, and widespread generalizations have been made on this basis. Recently, however, Green (1969) reported on an investigation concerned with the validity of the *responses* given and the actual *behavior* of respondents regarding the use and knowledge of contraceptives in East Pakistan. The data included both direct and behavioral measures (from the clinic and education program records) and the verbal reports of behavior from respondents. It was found that people underreported both their use and knowledge of contraceptives, although they were less reluctant to admit knowledge of family planning methods than they were to admit that they used the methods. About one out of five men and one out of four women who (according to education program records) knew of contraceptives denied any knowledge of them. Of all couples who had used contraceptives (as indicated by clinic records), about one out of every five husbands and one out of every three wives denied ever having used them. Although this study was done in East Pakistan, Green's findings raise important questions about the validity of people's responses to all survey studies concerned with the use of contraceptives.

Studies concerned with the accuracy of health information have also revealed discrepancies between people's reports to interviewers and hospital records. Cannell and Fowler (1963) found that 58 per cent of the respondents in their study gave inaccurate reports concerning their length of stay in the hospital, 23 per cent were inaccurate with regard to the month of discharge, 35 per cent with regard to diagnosis, 25 per cent with regard to type of surgery, and 10 per cent were inaccurate in their reports as to whether or not surgery had been performed.

People's reports on a wide variety of other measures have also been found to have varying degrees of validity. For example,

Robins (1963) determined in interviewing a sample consisting mainly of former patients of a child guidance clinic, for whom information from adult records was available, that 42 per cent of those who had adult nontraffic arrests failed to admit them, 29 per cent of those persons who had been truants as children denied it, 23 per cent of those who had not attended high school claimed that they were high school graduates or had attended college, and 13 per cent of those who were divorced denied the fact. C. Weiss (1968) found that 37 per cent of the responses from her sample of welfare mothers were inaccurate with respect to whether a child had received a failing mark on the last report card. Cahalan (1968) reports that among individuals constituting his sample of Denver adults, 10 per cent exaggerated the possession of a driver's license and 34 per cent exaggerated their contributions to a recent Community Chest drive. And Larsen and DeFleur (1955) found that when people were asked to mail a postage-paid reply card in response to a leaflet drop, 93 per cent of those who said they had not mailed any card had, in fact, not done so. But only 53 per cent of those individuals who said they had done so could be verified.

Another area of investigation where there have been recent attempts at validation is that concerned with people's self-reports of various types of deviant behavior. In one of these investigations, Gould (1969) notes the failure of previous self-reports of delinquency to gather the kinds of data which would allow for the simultaneous comparison of officially reported and self-reported delinquency for the same individuals. Measuring self-reported delinquency through the use of a nine-item scale, Gould (1969:331) found a very weak relationship between these self-reports and various official reports. The level of correlation (gamma) was .16 with juvenile court and police court records, and .10 with counselor ratings and school records. Gould (1969:332) concludes that

self-reported measures of delinquency are not good measures of the incidence and distribution of delinquent acts in the population. . . . They do not, for example, include the whole range of acts which are against the law, and the items which are included are generally of a less serious nature than the things which account for most official delinquency.

In addition, self-reported indices of delinquency suffer from problems of recall and candor.

It should be emphasized that Gould's results show that self-reports of delinquency are not valid measures of *official* reports of delinquency. This does not, of course, answer the question as to whether these self-report measures are valid indicators of the delinquent acts which people actually have committed. There is, however, a recent study which is concerned with this latter issue. In that study, Clark and Tifft (1966) first asked people to check whether or not they had ever engaged in each of thirty-five different deviant behaviors. They then asked these same individuals to submit to a polygraph ("lie detector") examination. Prior to their taking the examination, each person was interviewed and told that he could select his questionnaire and make whatever modifications (in private) were necessary to achieve 100 per cent accuracy. In the words of the authors (Clark and Tifft, 1966:520):

By the time the polygraph examinations were completed, all respondents had made corrections to their questionnaire responses. About 58 per cent of the total number of changes between the initial questionnaire responses and the final responses were made at the time of the personal "interview" and 42 per cent during the polygraph examination. Three-fourths of all changes increased the frequency of admitted deviance, the remainder were in the opposite direction. In fact, all respondents under-reported the frequency of their misconduct on at least one item but only one-half over-reported on at least one item.

While one may, of course, question the extent of polygraph validity, there is reason to believe that a properly administered polygraph has great accuracy (Clark and Tifft, 1966:519–520). If we accept the use of the polygraph as an appropriate validation technique, we must conclude that many people do not tell the truth about certain deviant behaviors when asked about them on questionnaires. For instance, of those whom the polygraph indicated "Had sex relations with a person of the same sex," only 14 per cent revealed this fact on the first questionnaire. Asked whether they had "Falsified information while filling out an application form or report," 43 per cent of those whom the polygraph showed had done so denied it initially. And of those whom the polygraph indicated had "masturbated," one-third initially failed to admit it.

Clark and Tifft (1966) attempted to locate some of the factors involved in these "systematic errors," as they termed them. They assumed that deviant behavior might be in conflict with either personal or group norms to which individuals usually conform. Therefore, the respondents were questioned about their feelings as to the acceptability of the behavior described in each of the items. In 66 per cent of the instances in which individuals did not initially admit an act but later did, they stated that the act was "never permissible" according to the perceived standards of their reference group. Clark and Tifft (1966:522) conclude from this that "there is strong evidence that errors on questionnaires are directly associated with perceived discrepancies between individual acts and personal and group norms. The errors represent an attempt to make reported behavior compatible with perceived norms." Clearly, this study shows that those items frequently used on delinquency scales are rather inaccurate, and it underscores the need for concern with the validity of self-reported measures of deviant behavior.

Another recent study concerned with the validity of certain measures of deviant behavior is reported by Ball (1967) who was concerned with the validity of interview data obtained from narcotic drug addicts. In this investigation, noninstitutionalized addicts' responses to questions regarding a number of topics were obtained in a situation where, according to Ball (1967), interviews were conducted by a highly competent and experienced interviewer with considerable knowledge of the addict subculture and of lower-class slum neighborhoods, who made it clear to the addicts that nothing was to be reported to the police. These data (which Ball implies were collected under maximally positive conditions) were then validated against such outside criteria as FBI records and urine specimens. The validation procedures revealed that about 20 per cent of the addicts reported their first arrests incorrectly and 30 per cent gave invalid reports of their criminal histories. Both of these reports were validated by FBI data, which may, of course, in themselves be inaccurate. However, the use of a chemical analysis of a urine specimen, which is regarded as the most valid physical means of ascertaining current opiate use, revealed that 29 per cent of those using heroin denied such use to the interviewer.

The studies cited above all underscore the fact that in many instances where a measure's validity can be checked against some outside criteria, the correlation between the measure and the criterion leaves much to be desired. It should be emphasized, however, that these validation studies are widely scattered throughout the social science literature. This means that the examples cited above are taken from some unknown universe of validation studies.

Although people's attitudes can be of interest in their own right, it is likely that many investigators who study attitudes are concerned with them mainly as they may relate to actual behavior. The evidence for the validity of attitude measures as they relate to behavior seems especially unimpressive. Beginning with LaPiere's (1934) finding that the actual willingness of hotels to serve a Chinese couple bore almost no relationship to the expressed willingness of hotel managers to serve such a couple, numerous studies (for example, Brookover and Holland, 1952; Dean, 1958; DeFleur and Westie, 1958; DeFriese and Ford, 1969; Freeman and Ataov, 1960; Hassinger and McNamara, 1957; Kutner et al., 1952; Linn, 1965; Lohman and Reitzes, 1954; Putney and Middleton, 1962; Saenger and Gilbert, 1950; Warriner, 1958) show vast discrepancies between what people say and what they do. Although a recent paper by Ehrlich (1969) argues that there is no necessary incompatibility between a theory of attitudes and theories of interpersonal or intergroup behavior, a reading of most attitudinal studies indicates that the researcher is usually interested in behavior rather than attitudes per se. Thus it seems to me that the lack of convergence between attitudes and behavior does, indeed, raise serious doubts about the validity of most attitudinal studies as measures directly translatable into behavior.

We have seen, then, that in instances where people's responses to social investigators' inquiries are checked against some outside criterion (voting registration records, the records of birth control clinics, lie detectors, chemical analyses of urine samples, etc.), the degree of fit is often far from perfect. And, in other instances, where the concern is with the relation between attitudes and actual behavior, the evidence shows that people's attitudes are often poor indicators of past behavior or predictors of future acts.[3]

We certainly cannot assume from this that all discrepancies between people's attitudes and actions are due to lying. Nor can we assume that all discrepancies between their responses and the facts regarding possession of a driver's license or being registered to vote, for example, are evidence of lying as a deliberate strategy. Undoubtedly, faulty memories, attempts to "take a stab" at answering questions which are not fully understood, and complete misunderstanding, all play a part. It is my view, however, that *conscious and deliberate* attempts on the part of respondents to deceive the investigator are far more prevalent than the other factors just mentioned. More will be said about this shortly.

VALIDATION IN TERMS OF MEASURES' ABILITY TO DISCRIMINATE

As was pointed out earlier, measures may be invalidated not only by showing that they correlate poorly with some outside criterion but also by showing that they correlate highly with some conceptually simpler variable or that they fail to discriminate the measure of interest from other measures.

This matter of the influence of nonrelevant variables in social research is an important one. For whatever the construct validity of an instrument, there are always nonrelevant response determinants which may influence people's reports and responses in sociological investigations. Hence, these variables may affect the validity of social science measures. Speaking of this problem as it pertains to attitude measures, Cook and Selltiz (1964:37) state that: "ideally, the goal would be to develop one or more measures from which the effects of all possible response determinants other than the attitude toward the relevant object would be removed." While a concern with removing these possible sources of bias is obviously an

---

[3] A recent, and very valuable, collection of papers concerning attitude studies is contained in Summers (1970).

important consideration, this must be preceded by an attempt to first *identify* the wide and varied assortment of factors which may undermine the validity of our measuring instruments. In the following presentation and discussion of some of these factors, evidence is drawn not only from survey studies, conducted mainly by sociologists, but also from laboratory and other investigations conducted by psychologists. All of these studies can be seen as involving different factors which may affect the discriminant validity of social science measures.

While any classification of the factors to be considered is, of necessity, arbitrary, it appears useful to categorize them in the following manner: (1) attributes of the interviewer and the experimenter, (2) subject and respondent attributes, (3) characteristics of physical settings, (4) investigator expectancy and modeling effects, and (5) miscellaneous biasing factors.

Interviewer and Experimenter Attributes

By now, there are several studies showing the effects of various attributes of the experimenter and interviewer on the responses and behavior of people in social science investigations. Among the strictly biological attributes considered in these studies are race, sex, and age.

Considering *race* first, Katz (1964) found that people's performances on various psychological tests are affected by the race of the experimenter. Rankin and Campbell (1955) reported that the galvanic skin response among whites showed a greater increase if the experimenter adjusting the apparatus was Negro rather than white. In survey studies, Hyman (1954) found that white interviewers received more proper or acceptable responses from their Negro respondents than did Negro interviewers, and Athey (1960) found that Negro and Oriental interviewers obtained more socially acceptable answers to questions concerning racial issues such as housing and intermarriage than did white interviewers. Similar evidence is presented in a study by Summers and Hammonds (1966), which employed a group-administered, anonymous, self-enumerated procedure. In a portion of the groups, both investigators were white; in the remainder, there were a white and a Negro investigator. It was found that when both investigators were white, 52 per cent of the respondents showed themselves to be highly prejudiced. When one of the investigators was Negro, however, 37 per cent were equally prejudiced. Just as Hyman (1954) found that Negro respondents said the "right" things more often to white interviewers, so too do white respondents apparently say the right thing to Negro interviewers (Athey, 1960) and when they fill out a questionnaire in the presence of a Negro investigator (Summers and Hammonds, 1966). Another study finding that the race of the interviewers was related to interview bias is reported by Williams (1964) who found that Negro respondents appeared more "honest" when interviewed by Negroes than when they were interviewed by whites.

There is also evidence pertaining to the *sex* of experimenters and interviewers on people's responses (Binder et al., 1957; Friedman, 1967; Sarason and Harmatz, 1965; Stevenson and Allen, 1964; Stevenson and Odom, 1963). For example, the study by Binder et al. (1957) found that a husky male experimenter described as an ex-marine obtained far poorer learning from his subjects than did an attractive female experimenter. In survey research, Benney and his associates (1956) found that when respondents were given an opportunity to assess the cause of abnormal behavior, they gave sexual interpretations 25 per cent more often when the interviewer was of their own, rather than the opposite, sex.

Turning now to the influence of *age*, Ehrlich and Riesman (1961) show that when adolescent girls are interviewed by female interviewers, both the respondents' and the interviewers' ages influence the girls' willingness to say socially unacceptable things. And Benney and his colleagues (1956) found that sex and age, considered together, influenced their respondents' willingness to speak frankly about matters of a sexual nature. The least inhibited communication took place between people of the same sex; the most inhibited between people of the same age but different sexes.

Religion and *social status*, two psychosocial attributes, also influence people's behavior in social investigations. For instance, Robinson and Rohde (1946) found that both whether interviewers looked Jewish and whether they gave Jewish names influenced greatly the extent of anti-Semitic responses in public opinion research. With regard to social status, Rosenthal (1966:76–77) summarizes the studies relevant to the experimenter's status by observing that:

> when the subject's task involves conforming to an experimenter's influence (as in studies of verbal conditioning by hypnosis), higher status experimenters are more successful in obtaining such conformity. This seems to be the case whether the experimenter's status is defined in terms of such external symbols as dress or insignia or in terms of status-earning behavior during the interaction with the subject.

Lenski and Leggett (1960) examined the effects of socio-economic discrepancies between interviewers and respondents, and found that Negro respondents and respondents of low status expressed deference to the middle-class interviewer by acquiescing to simple agree-disagree type propositions, even when the two propositions were contradictory to one another. An earlier study by Katz (1942) also showed that social class disparities between interviewers and respondents produced biases in responses. Riesman's (1958) investigation of the interviewing of academic elites can be seen as suggesting that academics may have been influenced in their interviews both by whether they were at leading or lesser institutions and by whether they were interviewed by market research or blue-stocking type interviewers. Dohrenwend et al. (1968) found that interviewers who preferred high-status respondents were more likely to bias respondents' answers in a mental health survey than were interviewers with no status preference.

Along with the effects of these variables, there are also the influences of certain *personality characteristics* of experimenters and interviewers. For example, there is some evidence to show that the subject's performance in a laboratory situation may be influenced by the anxiety level of the experimenter (Cleveland, 1951; McGuigan, 1963; Winkel and Sarason, 1964). Other studies show that the experimenter's need for social approval may influence his subjects' responses in laboratory experiments (Mulry, 1962). And the experimenter's hostility (Sarason, 1962), authoritarianism (Mulry, 1962), and perceived warmth (Luft, 1953; Sampson and

French, 1960) all appear to exercise some influence on subjects' behavior in the laboratory. Unfortunately, no investigations were uncovered in which interviewers' personality attributes were examined for their effects on people's responses in survey studies.

Subject and Respondent Attributes

In addition to the influence of qualities of the experimenter and the interviewer on people's responses, there are also, of course, the effects of certain attributes of the subject and respondent as well. Several investigators have spoken of the subjects' desire to please the investigator. Rosenberg (1965, 1969), for example, has been interested in "evaluation apprehension" which he defines (Rosenberg, 1969:281) as "an active, anxiety-toned concern that he [the subject] win a positive evaluation from the experimenter, or at least that he provide no grounds for a negative one." Rosenberg has shown that, once aroused, evaluation apprehension can significantly influence the dependent variables in much laboratory research. That is, it acts as a source of systematic bias with experimental subjects trying to behave in the way that they hypothesize will win them approval. Riecken (1962) spoke of something similar when he referred to the subject's desire to "put his best foot forward." Crowne and Marlowe (1964) have focused on the influence of people's "need for social approval" as it affects their responses in various task and test situations. Their research demonstrates that persons with a high need for social approval are more sensitive than others to perceived situational demands by the experimenter or investigator and are more likely to respond affirmatively to social influences, tending, for example, to terminate psychotherapy more quickly than persons with less need for social approval, and producing less revealing projective-test protocols.

"Acquiescent response set" is another individual attribute which has been found important in many studies, although sociologists almost never consider this variable in their research. Bass (1955), for example, has concluded that the F-scale used in measuring authoritarianism is really little more than a measure of acquiescence. And Messick and Jackson (1961) have shown that much of the variance in psychological instruments is attributable to an acquiescent response set on the part of subjects.[4] Related to this is the work of Couch and Keniston (1960) on "yeasayers" (those individuals who tend to say "yes" or agree when responding to personality and attitude scale items) and "naysayers" (those who tend to say "no" and disagree). That these response tendencies may be relevant to people's reports in survey studies is indicated by a recent investigation by Wells (1963) who was concerned with people who overclaim in surveys. He found that 69 per cent of the yeasayers and only 18 per cent of the naysayers made at least one unsubstantiated claim about the possession in their home of various popular magazines.

Another type of response bias studied by psychologists involves social desirability the tendency of people to deny socially undesirable traits and to admit socially desirable ones. According to Edwards (1959), much of the variance in all self-inventories of personality can be explained by the social desirability variable. He states: "whenever we have a personality inventory in which the items in the inventory vary with respect to their social desirability scale values, we may expect to find a substantial positive correlation between probability of endorsement of an item and social desirability scale value of the item."

Physical Settings

Although little research has been done as to the effects of physical settings on people's responses in either laboratory or survey studies, there are two investigations which are informative on this matter. In the first of these, Maslow and Mintz (1956) were concerned with the short-term effects of three visual-esthetic conditions—"beautiful," "average," and "ugly" rooms—upon people's judgments of 10 photographs. For each photograph, people were asked to rate them as to their "energy" and "well-being." Individuals in the beautiful room gave significantly higher ratings (that is, they attributed more energy and greater well-being) to the photographs than those in the other two rooms. In the second study (Mintz, 1956), the male and female examiners who had gathered

---

[4] For a contrary view, see the paper by Rorer (1965).

the ratings in the above study were, although they did not know it, themselves the object of investigations. Over a period of three weeks, they spent prolonged sessions testing individuals in the "beautiful" and the "ugly" room. During the three-week period, the examiners in the beautiful room consistently gave higher ratings to the photographs. Generally, an examiner in the ugly room finished testing more quickly than an examiner in the beautiful room. The examiners' observational notes (Mintz, 1956:466) showed that in the ugly room the examiners "had such reactions as monotony, fatigue, headache, sleep, discontent, irritability, hostility and avoidance of the room," while in the beautiful room they "had feelings of comfort, pleasure, enjoyment, importance, energy, and a desire to continue their activity." Mintz concludes that visual-esthetic surroundings (at least as represented by beautiful and ugly rooms) can have significant effects upon persons exposed to them in a testing situation. While similar effects may exist for different interviewing sites in survey research, no studies pertaining to this possibility have been uncovered.

Expectancy and Modeling Effects

There are a number of recent studies concerned with the extent to which the laboratory experimenter may, quite unintentionally, suggest or convey to the subject *his own* appraisal of the experimental stimulus. These suggestions to the subject, of course, affect the results of the experiment. Rosenthal (1966) reports on a series of nine experiments designed to assess the occurrence and magnitude of these "modeling effects." as he calls them, in laboratory settings. Modeling effects were defined by the correlations between the mean ratings of various photographs by the different experimenters themselves and the mean photo ratings obtained by each experimenter from all subjects. From these studies, it was concluded that the subjects' ratings were strongly correlated with the ratings given by the experimenter.

   Another related concern of Rosenthal (1966) is with "experimenter expectancy." Rosenthal wanted to determine to what extent the results an experimenter obtains from his subjects are influenced by what he expects of them. The most general statement that can be made about his presentation is to observe that experimenters' expectancies as to subjects' performances have a strong influence on the subjects' actual performances. This is true not only for the performance of human subjects, but for animal subjects as well. In one study (Rosenthal and Fode. 1963). a group of experimenters was informed that their rats had been bred so that they were "maze-bright" (intelligent) and a second group of experimenters was told that they had "maze-dull" rats. The results of this study revealed that experimenters who believed that their rats were bright obtained a performance from them that was significantly superior to that obtained by experimenters who believed that their subjects (rats) were dull. even though both groups of rats were actually of equal intelligence.

Although we cannot be sure how the experimenters' expectancies were communicated to the rats, Rosenthal (1966:165) offers the following explanation:

> Rats are sensitive to visual, auditory, olfactory, and tactual cues. These last, the tactual, were perhaps the major cues mediating the experimenter's expectancy to the animal. . . . Experimenters expecting and obtaining better performances handled their rats more and also more gently than did the experimenters expecting and obtaining poorer performance.

There has been far less concern with expectancy effects in survey studies than in laboratory experiments. But a few studies do deal with this issue. An early investigation by Stuart Rice (1929) concerned 2,000 applicants for charity, each of whom was interviewed by one of twelve trained interviewers. He reported that one of the interviewers, who was known to be a staunch prohibitionist, obtained three times as many responses blaming alcohol as did another interviewer regarded as a socialist. The socialist interviewer, in turn, obtained half again as many responses blaming industrial factors as did the prohibitionist interviewer. Rice felt that the expectancy of the interviewer was in some way conveyed to the respondent, who then answered as expected. Other early studies which found expectancy effects are reported by Harvey (1938) and by Wyatt and Campbell (1950). Unfortunately, these studies do not allow us to determine whether it was the effects of the interviewers' expectancies or errors and cheating in recording responses which led to the results. But, in either case, the interviewers did affect the results obtained.

The most interesting question raised by the studies cited above is: How does the investigator inform his subject what it is he expects of him? What are the cues or clues which are conveyed to him? Analyses of several films of the laboratory situation by Friedman (1967) and Rosenthal (1966), while interesting and worthwhile, have only begun to locate the specific signals by which experimenters communicate their expectancies to their subjects.[5]

Miscellaneous Biasing Factors

Attributes of experimenters, interviewers, subjects, and respondents are not the only factors which influence what goes on in the laboratory or in the interview situation. For instance, Dohrenwend et al. (1968) and Williams (1964, 1968) found that respondent bias was affected by the "social distance" between interviewer and respondent. Brown (1955) examined the effects of interviewers' "rapport" in survey settings and found that fewer "don't know" responses and a greater number of usable replies to open-ended questions are associated with higher rapport. Carol Weiss (1968), on the other hand, found that the better the rapport between interviewer and respondent, the greater the proportion of biased responses. For example, the extent of bias with regard to being registered to vote was 26 per cent with "confiding" rapport, 14 per cent with "frank" rapport, and only 2 per cent with "poor" rapport.

Another source of bias concerns the experimenter's analysis of early data returns, which Rosenthal (1966) discovered affects subsequently obtained data. Rosenthal (1966:203) speculates as follows about these results: "When the early returns of an experiment are 'good,' the hypothesis with which the experimenter undertook the study is partially confirmed in his own mind and thereby

---

[5] A fascinating, but inconclusive, exchange of views on this matter of modeling and expectancy effects is found in Barber and Silver (1968a, 1968b) and Rosenthal (1968).

strengthened, with a possible increase in the biasing phenomenon for subsequent subjects." Although no evidence from survey studies seems to be available, we can easily imagine something similar occurring in the early analyses of survey data.

All of the above variables can be seen as exercising an effect on a great variety of measures of interest to social science, and they all probably lower the validity of social science measuring instruments. They all, therefore, raise questions about the *discriminant* validity of various measures. While they may all affect the validity of our measures, not all may exercise a *systematic* influence on these measures. That is, it is not enough to establish a relationship between any one of these variables and measures of the dependent variables considered in the above discussion: for example, racial attitudes, mental health, laboratory tasks, and authoritarianism. For to constitute a *systematic bias,* the variable contributing to the invalidity of a measure must be related both to that measure and to the independent variable of principal interest. If a tendency toward naysaying, for instance, is related both to people's education level *and* to their expressed attitudes toward Negroes, then naysaying can be said to exercise a systematic bias affecting the relationship between education level and racial attitudes. If, on the other hand, naysaying is related to attitudes toward Negroes but is distributed randomly among groups with differing educational levels, it clearly does not constitute a systematic bias—although the validity of the measure of racial attitudes is affected. Or, if expectancy effects in laboratory studies relate both to a dependent variable like task performance and to an independent variable such as sex, then there is a systematic bias, while if expectancy effects are related to task performance but not to sexual status there is no bias. If, as a final example, a survey were concerned with people's ages and their attitudes toward various sexual practices, and people's responses were influenced by the sex of the person interviewing them, then a bias would exist *only* if the different age groups were interviewed disproportionately by male or female interviewers.

The possibility of systematic biases has long been recognized by sociologists, but the tendency has always been to assume that these biases are random rather than systematic. For example, Hyman (1954:221) notes that:

although there is undoubtedly a good deal of random or situational error in interviews, it still seems very possible that different interviewers may exert differential net biases on given respondents or subgroups of respondents. These individual biases may cancel out to a large extent when the total assignment per interviewer contains a number of respondents or a number of groups of respondents.

While this may be true with regard to the marginal frequency distributions obtained, if the errors *are* systematic it will not be true for more refined analyses. In a situation where the independent variables of principal concern to the sociologist are able to account for such a small amount of the variance in his dependent variables, it seems especially important that serious consideration be given to other variables salient to data-collection activities which may affect the results of sociological investigations.

In the majority of studies concerned with the influence of various nonrelevant response determinants in social science investigations, the concern has been with the effects of these variables on certain measures and instruments, i.e., with the extent to which a measure is made less valid. For the most part, researchers have not asked whether certain relationships can be *explained* or *accounted for* by the presence of certain systematic biases. Since such a high percentage of sociological research involves the use of interviews in survey studies of various social phenomena, it is perhaps somewhat surprising that there have been so few studies concerned with some of the sources of bias discussed earlier. This reflects, of course, the general failure of sociologists to consider the validity of the measuring instruments which they employ. Yet, one would expect that especially in studies of so-called deviant behavior. sociologists would give greater attention to problems of bias. For instance, Maccoby and Maccoby (1954:482) remark that "when people are being interviewed (or are filling out questionnaires) directly concerning behavior about which there is a strong expectation of social approval or disapproval, and in which there is considerable ego-involvement, they tend to err in the direction of idealizing their behavior."

Let us consider, then, whether this tendency to err may be

related to people's location in the social structure. In considering this issue, I will use the example of mental illness to suggest that there are certain biases which relate both to characteristics of respondents and to behavior of interest to the sociological investigator.

As it has become more and more apparent that official records and statistics provide an unsatisfactory estimate as to the number of people who are what psychiatrists term mentally ill, investigators have increasingly turned to the utilization of other techniques for determining the true prevalence of mental illness in American society. Several studies have employed field interviews of nonhospitalized populations as a means of obtaining data concerning the quantity and quality of psychiatric disorders. Probably the best known of these investigations are the Midtown (Langner and Michael, 1963; Srole et al., 1962) and Stirling County studies (Leighton, 1959; Leighton et al., 1963). Among other investigations utilizing field interviews for estimating the prevalence of mental illness are those by Abrahamson (1966), Dohrenwend (1966), Gurin et al. (1960), Haberman (1963), Manis and his associates (1964), Phillips (1966), and Summers (1969).

While the Midtown and Stirling County investigations employed other measures as well, all of these true prevalence studies rely very heavily on the use of psychiatric inventories. These inventories consist of questions asking people: "Do you feel somewhat apart or alone even among friends?" "Do you feel that nothing turns out for you the way you want it to?" "Do you have personal worries that get you down physically?" In other words, psychiatric evaluations are made on the basis of people's responses to interviewers' inquiries regarding certain feelings, experiences, and behaviors that are considered by experts to be indicative of mental illness or malfunctioning. This means, of course, that figures concerning the true prevalence rates of mental illness in general populations ultimately rest on people's reporting or admitting to the kinds of symptoms contained in these inventories.

Mention was made earlier of Edwards' (1959) caution that whenever we employ an inventory in which the items vary with respect to their social desirability, we should expect less desirable items to be endorsed less frequently than those high on the scale of social desirability. Now, in the case of psychiatric inventories researchers are interested in (1) the respondent's *actual* feelings or experiences ("feeling apart among friends," feeling that "nothing turns out right," "personal worries," or whatever). But also involved in his responses are: (2) his knowledge of his own personal characteristics, and (3) his frankness in telling what he knows or feels. Only the last of the above, frankness, can be considered part of a social desirability response style in psychiatric inventories (Nunnally, 1967).

The question with psychiatric inventories, then, is whether the relationships between mental illness and certain other, independent variables to which it has been found to be related might be partially a result of a systematic bias: in this instance, a social desirability response set. As noted earlier, these inventories have been widely used—with the possibility of systematic bias being given little attention. There are, however, three different studies that are suggestive of the probable influence of the social desirability factor in investigations of mental health and illness.

The first of these studies was concerned with the relationship between sexual status and psychiatric symptoms. In this investigation, Phillips and Segal (1969) hypothesized that women would report more pyschiatric symptoms than would men with the same number of physical illnesses. We used the number of physical illnesses which people had as a rough indicator of stress, in that we wanted to compare the responses of men and women under approximately equal stress conditions. We reasoned that women would be likelier than men to *report* or *admit to* the kinds of acts, behaviors, and feelings that lead to their being categorized as mentally ill, *not* because women actually experienced them more often but rather because it is more culturally appropriate and acceptable in American society for women to be expressive about their difficulties. In other words, it was argued that these symptoms are less socially undesirable for women than for men and that, therefore, women would be more frank about them. While the results of our investigation (Phillips and Segal, 1969) were supportive of the above argument, there was one obvious gap in the study: we employed no independent measures as to what men and women saw as inappropriate or socially undesirable behavior for someone of their sexual status.

However, the second study of interest here does deal more adequately with this problem. This investigation by Dohrenwend (1966) used the same mental health inventory employed by Phillips and Segal. Dohrenwend too questioned the validity of the inventory and suggested that response biases may play an important role in determining the responses (and hence, the rates) obtained in studies using psychiatric inventories.

Dohrenwend's initial investigation was concerned mainly with the influence of people's social class position and ethnicity on their mental health status. After finding that with social class held constant, Puerto Ricans had a higher rate of mental illness (i.e., higher inventory scores) than Jews, Irish, or Negroes in a sample of New York City residents, Dohrenwend asked whether these differences in rates might not reflect culturally patterned differences in the modes of *expressing* distress and/or culturally patterned *willingness* to report or admit distress. To investigate further these possibilities, Dohrenwend asked a different group of respondents to rate the items in the psychiatric inventory as to their social desirability. This revealed that on seventeen of the twenty-two items constituting the inventory the Puerto Ricans gave a *less* undesirable rating than did the other three groups. Dohrenwend found some support, therefore, for his suggestion that because the Puerto Ricans regarded the characteristics in the mental health inventory as less undesirable than did members of the other ethnic groups they might also be more willing than the other groups to admit such characteristics. If this were true, then they may actually have a very much lower rate of mental illness than their reports on psychiatric inventories would suggest.

A matter of great importance here is the nature of the relationship between people's ethnicity and their evaluation of the desirability of the items in the mental health inventory. Why is it that Puerto Ricans perceive the items as less undesirable than do the other ethnic groups? In an attempt to answer this question, Dohrenwend posits two alternative hypotheses. Following a line of reasoning outlined by Heilbrun (1964), he writes that since the Puerto

Ricans in his study regard the characteristics described in the mental health inventory as less undesirable than do members of other groups, it may be (Dohrenwend, 1966:24)

> that they would also be more willing than other groups, on this account, to admit such characteristics. If so, they may actually have a much lower rate of disorder than their rate of reported symptoms would suggest. On the other hand, the reason Puerto Ricans see these symptoms as less undesirable may be because they are actually more common among Puerto Ricans. If this is so, then higher rates of reported symptoms among Puerto Ricans and their lower tendency to see these symptoms as strongly undesirable may both indicate the same thing—higher actual rates of disorder.

Unfortunately, Dohrenwend's data did not allow him to choose between these two alternative hypotheses. But before discussing a third study (Phillips and Clancy, 1970) which did consider these alternatives, it is useful to give further attention to Dohrenwend's two hypotheses regarding the relationship between people's assessments as to the social desirability of the mental health inventory items and their inventory scores. Dohrenwend's first hypothesis suggests that one's evaluation as to the desirability of the inventory items can vary independently of the prevalence of the symptoms among members of one's own group, and that an individual's perceptions of what is or is not desirable can be determined by forces external to his traditional reference group of family, friends, or neighbors of similar socioeconomic and cultural background.

The second of Dohrenwend's hypotheses suggests that an individual comes to learn or perceive the desirability or undesirability of a given symptom by observing the *prevalence* of that symptom among people like himself, other persons of his ethnic and/or social class background. He argues that if symptoms are common among one's own status group—in this case, family, friends, and neighbors—then the desirability of the items will be higher than if the symptoms are not common.

This latter interpretation assumes that the social environment of an individual determines his evaluations as to the desirability of given symptoms, and that the most important aspect of this social environment is the actual (or perhaps, more properly, the perceived) prevalence of these symptoms among a man's traditional reference group. This may or may not be the case, for his line of reasoning does not account for the efforts of some Negroes to "pass," the striving of the Irish, Negroes, Germans, Italians, Jews, and now, Puerto Ricans, to lose their native accents, nor for other similar everyday instances where members of a given group seem to consider characteristics highly common within that group to be undesirable.

In an attempt to choose between the two hypotheses offered by Dohrenwend, Kevin Clancy and I engaged in an investigation in which we predicted that: (1) People's scores on the twenty-two-item mental health inventory used by Dohrenwend (1966), Phillips and Segal (1969), and other investigators would be related to their assessments of the desirability of the items. This was, of course, stated by Dohrenwend, although he did not have data on social desirability ratings and inventory scores from *the same persons*. Rather he found that Puerto Ricans had both higher symptom scores and saw the items as less undesirable than did other groups —but he had no data regarding individual comparisons. (2) People's assessments as to the desirability of the inventory items would reflect something other than the estimated prevalence of these symptoms within their traditional reference groups. Thus, it was expected that people's assessments as to the desirability of the items and their estimates of the prevalence of such symptoms would be independent predictors of scores on the symptom inventory. (3) A final concern of the study was with determining the extent to which the three variables discussed above—assessment of social desirability, estimated prevalence, and psychiatric inventory scores—were related to people's actual social class position.

We found (Phillips and Clancy, 1970) that our first hypothesis was supported by the data; the more undesirable people's evaluations of the inventory items, the fewer symptoms they reported. With regard to the second hypothesis, we found that people's assessments regarding the desirability of the items were independently related to both their estimates of prevalence and their social class positions. The greater their estimates as to the prevalence of similar symptoms within their reference groups and the lower their positions in the social class hierarchy, the larger the number of symptoms reported. Furthermore, the independent effects of these two variables on assessments regarding social desirability were of about equal magnitude.

What this means, then, is that people's views concerning the desirability or undesirability of the psychiatric inventory items seem to be, as Dohrenwend suggested, determined partially by their looking around and making a judgment as to how many of their "significant others" show similar characteristics. But people's views with regard to the desirability of certain behaviors and experiences are also influenced by their class location.

In that people's assessments concerning the desirability of the psychiatric inventory items are dependent partially on their positions in the class structure, and since their scores on the inventory are strongly related to their assessment of the items' desirability, it may be that the frequently demonstrated inverse relationship between social class position and mental health (Dohrenwend, 1966; Gurin et al., 1960; Langner and Michael, 1963; Leighton et al., 1963; Phillips, 1966; Summers, 1969; Srole et al., 1962) might be accounted for largely by the above-mentioned social class differentials in people's assessments as to the social desirability of the items constituting mental health inventories. That is, it may be that the reason that lower-class persons appear to have so many symptoms of poor mental health is not, as has so frequently been argued, due entirely to a greater quantity of stresses and strains associated with lower-class life, but is due rather to a greater willingness of lower-class persons to *admit to* or *report* certain behaviors and experiences which middle- and upper-class persons regard as highly undesirable. The data gathered by Phillips and Clancy (1970) lend strong support to this possibility. We found that when people's assessments as to item desirability were held constant, the magnitude of the relationship between social class and mental health status was reduced considerably. In fact, when the independent effects of the two variables—social class and social desirability—were compared, it was revealed that people's assessments of the desirability of the inventory items had a *greater* influence upon their inventory scores than did their social class position.

My study with Clancy has been discussed at some length because it is one of the few sociological investigations in which a possible biasing factor is given detailed attention and included as part of the analysis concerning a relationship between a study's chief independent and dependent variables. If, as that study has indicated, one response determinant (social desirability) can exercise such a profound effect on the relation between the variables of principal research interest in a survey study, we can imagine the possible cumulative effects of numerous other (unmeasured) response determinants in sociological investigations. However, rather than consider these other possible biasing factors (and their implications for social research) at the present time, I will now speculate about what occurs in field studies of mental illness in which data are collected from interviews with people of various socioeconomic backgrounds.

Consider, first, the question of whether people differ in their *knowledge* or *awareness* that psychiatric inventories contain questions pertaining to their mental health status. That is, are people's abilities to correctly define the interview situation as one in which they are being psychiatrically evaluated related in a systematic way to their location in the class structure? This is an important and difficult question for which no definitive answer is readily available. But it would seem reasonable to suggest such a relationship. Individuals occupying a high social class position are probably better able than others to see the interview situation as one in which their mental health is being assessed. Because of their greater education, they are more likely than people with less schooling to have encountered similar instruments and measures as part of the content of their schooling (in sociology and psychology courses, for instance), as well as having experienced these as part of the application procedure for college and for jobs. Not only are they more likely than less-educated and lower-class persons to have had experience with such instruments, but they are also more apt to have been apprised as to their purpose. As Gurin and others (1960) have noted, those with greater education are more psychologically sophisticated in general, and are also better able to recognize the signs and symptoms of mental illness. It seems correct to suggest, then, that there are class-linked differences in people's abilities to recognize that questions concerning nervousness, trouble sleeping, and so forth are being used as a means for estimating their mental health status. While these differences may also be systematically related to other variables such as age, sex, and ethnicity, it certainly seems correct to argue that they are highly likely to be related to socioeconomic status.

Consider, secondly, the matter of the implications of the responses which people make in psychiatric inventories. Here, too, it seems apparent that there are class-linked differences. Individuals with greater education, because of their greater psychological sophistication, are undoubtedly better able than other persons to recognize that their responses to the kinds of questions contained in psychiatric inventories may be put to a number of uses. In the case of their employment, for instance, they may be aware that replies to similar questions are frequently used as one basis for hiring, promotion, demotion, and firing. Similar class-associated differences in awareness probably exist when people respond to verbal inquiries or fill out questionnaires when applying for medical or life insurance, or for a license to drive an automobile or own a gun. That is, individuals of higher class standing are probably more apt to recognize that responding affirmatively to questions that may classify them as mentally ill is likely to have negative consequences for them. Persons of higher socioeconomic status, therefore, are more likely than others to have learned that the "correct," "right," or "best" answers regarding inquiries that appear to pertain to mental illness are those that deny any troubles or problems.

An example of providing the "right" answers to certain kinds of inventory questions is seen in the advice offered by Whyte, in *The Organization Man* (1956:179, 196–197), to men who must take personality tests:

> When an individual is commanded by an organization to reveal his inner-most feelings, he has a duty to himself to give answers that serve his self-interest rather than that

of the Organization. In a word, he should cheat. . . . When
in doubt about the most beneficial answer to any question,
repeat to yourself: I loved my father and my mother, but
my father a little bit more. I like things pretty much the
way they are. I never worry about anything.

In other words, Whyte is counseling people to decide what is the
safest answer on each inventory or test question and to give that
response.

If it is, indeed, true that many persons do lie or try to deceive
investigators when being interviewed, filling out a questionnaire,
or participating in a laboratory experiment, it raises several important questions. Do the same social processes operate in these data-
collection activities as in other everyday social activities? If so,
why do people frequently try to emit socially desirable (right, safe,
correct) behavior (by lying and acts of deception) in their interactions with others? And what are the various elements or factors
that people consider as a basis for determining the direction and
content of social interaction? That is, how do they decide what
is required or expected of them in various social situations? An
attempt to answer these questions is provided in the following
chapters.

Before we go on to Chapter III, however, I want to suggest
some implications of the materials dealt with in the present chapter.
What we have seen is that the *collecting* of sociological and psychological data does exert an influence on the results obtained.
This means that despite all that has been written about the *objectivity* of certain methods for data collection, the social sciences are
far from achieving that end. Consider this in terms of three ideals
which social scientists often stress as important to their research:
controlled data-collection procedures, the replication of procedures, and the cumulation of results.

The principal methods of data collection and analysis in sociology (interviews and questionnaires) and psychology (laboratory
experiments) have as their model the controlled experiment as
found in the natural sciences. In the laboratory experiment, an
experimental group is exposed to the independent variable of
chief interest while the control group is not; the two groups are

then compared in terms of the effects on some dependent variable. Randomization in the assignment of subjects to the two groups controls the effects of confounding variables. With studies using interviews and questionnaires, however, the control of confounding or extraneous variables usually comes about in one of two ways: (1) the sample is selected in such a way that certain factors do not operate as variables; e.g., only men may be included in the sample, or only persons under age forty; (2) in the analysis of the data, certain variables are held constant; e.g., the relationship between religious affiliation and voting preference might be examined within each of several social class divisions.

In the types of controlled empirical inquiries described above, the ideal is that *no* variables other than those of explicit theoretical and empirical interest will affect the results. This means that there should be no uncontrolled influences by other subject or respondent variables, situational factors, or attributes of the data collector. Obviously, perfect control, in the sense described here, is impossible. But what is important is that unintended variations in data-collection procedures be of minor magnitude, that they be generally irrelevant to a subject's responses, and, that when unintended variations do occur, they not be systematic. My review of the literature in the past several pages is meant to suggest that much (in my view, most) social science research falls considerably short of this ideal of controlled procedures.

Since we do not have controlled data-collection procedures, it is extremely difficult to achieve the goal of replication. While the sociologist or psychologist may make explicit a description of such things as the content of the interview or questionnaire, the exact words that were read from the instructions, and the way in which the data were analyzed, this does not constitute replication. For if another investigator were to try to reproduce the first man's data-collection procedures, he would, among other things, have to obtain interviewers who possessed the same relevant qualities (in the same combinations or mixes) as those who did the original interviewing. If the intent of replication is not to vary *anything* which makes a *difference* in people's responses, then replication is very much more difficult than is usually acknowledged.

Friedman's (1967:150) remarks on the replication of psychological experiments are relevant here. He notes that

> psychologists do not, as a rule, report how many glances they exchanged with their subjects while reading the instructions, nor would they have any way of knowing if they decided to. Nor do they, as a rule, report the exact duration of each phase of each experimental session. Hence, working from the public description of the experiment, it is unlikely that another experimenter would replicate the exchange of glances variable or the time variable.

Should it be the case (as Friedman found) that the experimenter's glances *are* relevant to the subjects' responses and behavior, the failure to include these would constitute a significant omission in a replication study. To the extent, then, that data-collection procedures are not controlled and not reported, they are not replicable.

What can be said about the cumulation of results? Obviously studies which are based on the utilization of procedures which are neither controlled nor replicable will not provide for empirical results that can in some way be added up or built upon.

The assumption by many social scientists that they can engage in research without influencing what they obtain in the way of data is preposterous. Despite the claims of many that our data collecting is objective, our procedures public, our findings replicable and cumulative, the evidence suggests the contrary. Much more will be said about objectivity and other issues relating to the strength and limitations of various data-collection procedures in the final chapters of this book. Thus we will postpone further consideration of these matters for the time being, and turn our attention to Chapter III which deals with social processes in everyday activities.

Chapter III

Social Processes
in Everyday Interaction:
A Brief Review

In the previous chapter, I discussed a number of studies in which various sources of bias, and possible invalidity, were considered. Among these were such biological characteristics as race, sex, and age; psychosocial attributes like religion and social status; personality characteristics such as evaluation apprehension, need for social approval, and acquiescence; differences in physical settings; and expectancy and modeling effects in the relationship between data collectors and subjects. All of these factors have been found to systematically affect the results of various measurement procedures. That is, people's responses or behaviors with respect to a number of different objects of measurement (racial prejudice, deviant behavior, magazine readership, laboratory task performance) are found to be due partially to differences among them on the variable of principal interest and partially to the systematic effects of other variables in the situation.

From the viewpoint of the researcher, all of the above-mentioned factors constitute sources of bias in his measurement procedures.

However, from a broader perspective, they constitute the very stuff which makes human interaction and communication possible. For they all represent situational stimuli which people may consider when in the presence of other persons. As Goffman (1959:1) puts it: "When an individual enters the presence of others, they commonly seek to acquire information about him or to bring into play information about him already possessed. . . . Information about the individual helps to define the situation, enabling others to know in advance what he will expect of them and what they may expect of him." On the basis of this information, the individual will tend to organize his behavior in light of what he feels the others expect is appropriate for someone like him in that kind of situation. He considers the meaning his behavior will have for others, he assesses his proposed behavior in light of the responses it will evoke in them, and then acts (or changes his actions) so as to achieve the anticipated responses that he wants. Other actors in the situation do the same. In short, people take account of one another in most social situations and act according to their definitions of the situation.

Now the above is almost a banality in the literature of sociology. For we all know that an individual's attitudes, opinions, and behavior are influenced by his perceptions and evaluations of the situations in which he finds himself. Despite the fact that we all know this, many sociologists seem unwilling to view the administration of an interview in a field survey or the filling out of a questionnaire as forms of social interaction—either real or symbolic. While Goode and Hatt (1952) state that "interviewing is a process of social interaction" and Hyman et al. (1954) note that the data obtained in the interview are "derived in an interpersonal situation," social researchers generally fail to take cognizance of the *extent* to which these "miniature social situations" (Hyman, 1949) are characterized by the same social processes that are found in other everyday activities. One writer who has recognized this is Riecken (1962:25) who states: "The process of collecting data about human behavior is itself a social process and shares features in common with other situations and events of human interaction."

Whenever one engages in social research, then, there will always exist what are (from the researcher's viewpoint) nonrelevant factors which influence the respondents' reports. Cicourel (1964: 79–80) states it this way:

> The respondents' and interviewers' stock of knowledge and their definitions of the situation will determine their mutual reaction to the questions posed. The relevancies not related to the substance of the interview *per se* will also determine the amount of extrainterview bias or error which exists. This is a necessary consequence of not treating each other only as objects for rational consideration; their attractiveness or unattractiveness to one another, their bodily presence, the social, physical, and role distance, all produce bias and error *naturally* because these are basic to the structure of everyday conduct.

If it is granted, as Riecken and Cicourel emphasize, that data-collection activities involve the same relevancies and the same social processes found in other social situations, then our next step should be to examine these relevancies and processes as they exist in other social situations. The main focus of this chapter, therefore, is on briefly considering some of the myriad factors that come into play when people confront one another. My intention in considering these factors is to underscore my belief that those elements which, from one point of view, constitute biases in sociological investigations, from another point of view, are part and parcel of social life. Thus, the social scientist should not be surprised that such factors play a part in his data-collection activities. Rather, his surprise would be more appropriate if these elements lay dormant and played *no* part in his relations with those studied. Once I have spelled out some of these features of human interaction in everyday social encounters, I will turn, in the following chapter, to a consideration of how some of these same features may operate in survey studies of social phenomena.

BACKGROUND ASSUMPTIONS

Whether they admit it or not, sociologists—like all men—view the behavior of themselves and others in terms of certain assumptions about man, about society, and about men in interaction with one another. This means that sociologists will organize their research and their writings in terms of such prior assumptions. It could not, of course, be otherwise. For like those whom he studies and writes about, the sociologist is influenced by his own experiences. Some sociologists undoubtedly will argue that they make no assumptions about man and society, or that their assumptions are supported by empirical evidence. In my view, this is hogwash. Little of what we think we know about the nature of man and society is based on *empirical* evidence.

Take, as an example, my discussion of what occurs when two people come together. Implicit in that discussion is a general view of man, what he is really like, or, in short a *model* of man. If I assert, for instance, that, "in order for interaction in the fullest sense to take place there must be communication between the actors in the social situation," my assertion suggests that this is indeed known to be the case. Unfortunately, there is very little agreement among sociologists as to such principles of social behavior and interaction. The reason for this reflects a fundamental problem in sociology: *What we know about social behavior is dependent on our methods for studying it, while our methods for studying it are dependent upon what we know about social behavior.* This suggests, then, that in order to know more about social behavior and interaction, we need better methods; and to obtain better methods, we need to know more about behavior and interaction. This constitutes a kind of vicious circle which we must break out of if sociology is to move beyond its present stage of development.

Clearly, the fact that we have neither adequate methodologies nor basic principles of social behavior has not prevented sociologists from theorizing about social phenomena or from engaging in social research. One reason for this is that all sociologists are guided in their work by *some* view of man, both with regard to his nature and the way he operates as a social actor. However, these views are seldom made explicit—although they can easily be seen in the interpretations which different sociologists offer as an attempt to make sense of the results of various studies. Given the task of offering an explanation for some pattern of association between two variables, it is likely that there would be little agreement among the explanations which different sociologists would put forth.

This lack of agreement among sociologists as to a model of the actor seems to be one of the realities which we are going to have to accept and live with. What we do not have to accept, however, is the failure of most sociologists to make explicit *their* views of the social actor. I fully recognize that much sociological research has as its goal the discovery of basic principles of social interaction, but I also believe that the character of that research reflects a good deal of what the sociologist already believes or assumes about man, the actor. To some extent these beliefs and assumptions are made explicit in such writings as the appendix to Whyte's *Street Corner Society* (1955), in Hammond's *Sociologists at Work* (1964), and in the introductory chapter of Lenski's *Power and Privilege* (1966).

Obviously, I have been leading up to a presentation of my own views concerning the nature of man and of men in interaction. While I have expressed dismay about the failure of most sociologists to be explicit on this matter, I should acknowledge that my own efforts to do so will not be wholly adequate. As Goffman (1969:3) points out, "assumptions about human nature . . . are not easy to uncover because they can be as deeply taken for granted by the student as by those he studies." Nevertheless, my presentation should provide the reader with a better idea than is usually the case as to some of a writer's assumptions and beliefs. I will state these as if they were universal truths, for an assumption unstated is one that cannot be criticized and cannot be submitted to the test of evidence. Hopefully, this will allow for more informed consideration and criticism of the materials to be dealt with in the remainder of this book.

To begin with, I view man as basically a self-centered being whose actions are guided by considerations of self-interest. Man acts to maximize certain, to him, pleasurable experiences and to minimize, again to him, unpleasurable experiences. This obviously does not mean that I believe that man has no concern for others, but rather his concern for them results from his feeling better (more virtuous, generous, or whatever) by engaging in behavior that aids others. My position is clearly stated by Lenski (1966:30) who offers the following as one of his basic postulates about the nature of man:

"When men are confronted with important decisions where they are obliged to choose between their own, or their group's, interests and the interests of others, they nearly always choose the former—though often seeking to hide this fact from themselves and others." While this may strike the reader as simply a version of the most simple form of hedonism, nevertheless, it fully represents my view.

Secondly, I believe that if we are to begin to understand what goes on when people come together, we should give some consideration to the *needs* which people have and which they try to have realized in their everyday interactions with other persons. One of the most remarkable things about present-day American sociology is the almost complete absence in the literature of any sustained discussion and consideration of human needs. There is a good deal of concern with such concepts as "significant others," "reference groups," "values," and "social norms"—all of which are utilized to help explain various types of social phenomena. But the arguments in which these concepts are contained seldom tell us *why* people behave as they do. To say, for example, that people vote as they do because of the influence of reference groups, that they have high birth rates because of religious values, or that they use alcohol because of the norms of the groups to which they belong, is to go only part way in terms of explanations of social phenomena. For the question still remains as to *how* reference groups, values, and norms exert an influence on people's behavior.

It is possible to go a step further and make explicit certain psychological assumptions that are left unstated in most sociological explanations. Before doing so, however, it is useful to comment on the great fear among some sociologists that if it should be shown that the ultimate basis of certain explanations about human behavior lies with propositions of a psychological nature, this will undermine their claims to a special expertise regarding social phenomena. This fear, as Homans (1964, 1967) has repeatedly demonstrated, is without foundation. Even if certain sociological propositions could be deduced from more general propositions that were psychological in character, this would not reduce all sociology to psychology. For it seems clear that a focus on the foundations of social institutions, on the relationships of institutions to one another, and on the development historically of different institutions is largely dependent upon sociological rather than psychological modes of analysis. However, I would still contend that any theories resulting from such analyses are what Homans calls "open at the top": that is, their highest order propositions are ultimately derivable from psychological propositions. Nor is there any substance to such assertions as a recent one by Robin Williams (1969:25) that "if we really want to be reductionists, why not go to neurology, biochemistry, and genetics." Why not, indeed? If enough were known to reduce certain psychological propositions to, for instance, genetics, this would be fine. It would not, however, reduce psychology to genetics.

In considering the relationship between norms and the use of alcohol, a rather common sociological explanation would take the following form. The reason that the rate of alcohol usage is higher at, say, Dartmouth than at Swarthmore is that drinking is a strongly held norm at Dartmouth but not at Swarthmore. In discussing this explanation, an attempt might be made to determine how the norms came to be as they are at the two institutions. But seldom would there be an explicit attempt to provide a linkage between the campuses' norms and people's behavior. However, such a linkage could be provided. It would look something like this.

Individuals whose behavior deviates from the norms of the group frequently threaten those who conform to the norms. People who are threatened are likely to punish (or fail to reward) those who threaten them. In the case of drinking behavior, the punishment might take various forms: ignoring the deviant, spending less time with him, poking fun at him, or whatever. The severity of the punishment is, of course, dependent on how strongly a norm is held; the more strongly it is held, the more severe the punishment is likely to be for those who break it. With individuals who deviate from the campus norms concerning the use of alcohol (probably not a very strongly held norm), it seems likely that what the punishment will consist of, in one form or another, is the withdrawal of social approval from the deviant. The deviant's punishment may result in his not being asked to parties, being denied dates, left out of bull sessions, and so on. Ultimately, though, all signify the same thing: a loss of social approval.

To go back, then, to the question of why so many more students drink at Dartmouth than at Swarthmore, we no longer have to settle for an explanation that tells us it is because of the norms. Rather, we now have a more complete explanation, one which says that they use alcohol because they would suffer a loss of *social approval* if they did not. Clearly, this explanation has not been spelled out in full—although it could be. But it is a fuller and more adequate explanation than that which simply involves the relationship between norms and conformity. This is, of course, the kind of explanation that Homans calls for and that, in my view, is necessary for sociology if it ever hopes to *explain* social phenomena.

One of the reasons that sociologists have avoided this type of explanation (in addition to their fear of being preempted by psychologists) is that it involves an explicit consideration of needs. As noted earlier, sociologists have long gone out of their way to avoid having to utilize such concepts as needs, motives, and drives in their explanations of social behavior, despite the fact that many sociologists frequently employ such concepts in their more casual interpretations and explanations of their own and other people's everyday behavior. This proclivity for avoiding such terms in their writings, taken together with an emphasis on avoiding psychological propositions, probably retards the sociologists' ability to formulate theories that explain social behavior and stand up to logical and empirical scrutiny.

Recently, however, a number of sociologists have explicitly dealt with the question of needs in their writings. Homans (1961, 1964), Blau (1964), Lenski (1966), and Etzioni (1968) have all recognized the necessity for considering needs in many explanations of social phenomena. Each of these writers has emphasized, in one way or another, the existence of a basic human need for social approval. Blau (1964:62) notes that: "men are anxious to receive social approval for their decisions and actions, for their opinions and suggestions. The approving agreement of others helps to confirm their judgments, to justify their conduct, and to validate their beliefs." Obviously, a serious problem with social approval, or any other social need, is that of obtaining evidence to show that it really is a basic, though socially acquired, human need. The gathering of such evidence is indeed difficult, although Etzioni (1968) has offered some suggestions as to how this might be accomplished.

It should be emphasized that in speaking of the need for social approval, I use the terms very loosely to include an individual's desire for love, attention, affection, praise, acceptance, and other positive evaluations from his fellow human beings. My emphasis is on social approval, broadly defined, as an important factor in most social activities. People strive to gain the approval of others and to avoid their disapproval. I am not arguing that social approval is the *only* social need that men have, although I do think it is probably the most basic of his socially acquired needs.[1] In discussions later on, I will suggest other needs that play a part in man's behavior. My point here, however, is that men do mutually seek approval from one another. In Linton's (1945:91) words: "the need for eliciting favorable responses from others is an almost constant component of [personality]. Indeed, it is not too much to say that there is very little organized human behavior which is not directed toward its satisfaction in at least some degree."

Thirdly, I assume that man is free to choose among whatever alternatives are seen as available to him. Granted that people often must choose from what are to them almost equally undesirable paths of action, and granted, men must always act on the basis of inadequate information, nonetheless, men always have the freedom to choose among whatever alternatives they perceive as available to them. In a sense. then, men are always responsible for their actions. Obviously, the choices which people perceive as available to them are dependent upon their location in the social structure, but still they must choose To deny that one has a choice, to pretend a voluntary act is necessary, is to be guilty of what Sartre (1956) calls "bad faith." As Berger (1963:144) points out, men "are in 'bad faith' when they attribute to iron necessity what they themselves are choosing to do."

A fourth assumption is that most social encounters are marked by social exchange. While Homans' (1961) writings on "exchange theory" deal almost entirely with enduring relationships, I regard

---

[1] For a somewhat different view, see Wrong (1961).

the same processes as occurring in many other face-to-face confrontations. To attain various goals (survival, health, prestige, wealth, social approval), men engage in exchange processes. Work is exchanged for money, money for health care, etc. Similarly, social interaction, in my view, consists of an exchange involving such social rewards as esteem, admiration, and respect. These exchanges also involve certain costs such as boredom, embarrassment, and expenditure of time.

Finally, as will become clear from much of what I have to say in the remainder of this chapter, I share many (but, I hasten to add, not all) of Erving Goffman's views concerning men's behavior in the presence of other men. Like Goffman, I see individuals as frequently involved in a "performance" which Goffman (1959:15) defines as "all the activity of a given participant on a given occasion which serves to influence in any way any of the other participants." In Goffman's view, when individuals come together, they ordinarily seek to acquire information about one another or to utilize whatever information about one another is already possessed. The sources of this information are "sign-vehicles" which are of two kinds: signs *given* and signs *given-off*. Signs are "given" through linguistic means, and are "given-off" expressively. While I make no effort to consistently employ Goffman's terminology in this report, I share many of his views of what occurs when people are physically in the presence of others. Like Goffman, I accept as a principle of social behavior that when an individual appears before others he generally has certain motives for trying to control the impression they receive of the situation. At least this is the case in those instances where the individual is concerned, interested, or invests himself in the social situation (Goffman, 1963).

Where I differ with Goffman is in his apparent view that individuals are *always* concerned with presenting a convincing image to others, that they are *always* concerned with controlling the image which others have of them. I prefer to think of man as always facing two kinds of problems: one, the problem of maintaining inner harmony with himself; the other, the problem of maintaining harmony with the social environment in which he finds himself. In either case, however, man's behavior is a function of his assessments as to the rewards or gratifications associated with one or another line of activity. This means that men will sometimes forego harmony with the social environment in order to achieve or preserve inner harmony. They may act for reasons of certain internalized norms—duty or loyalty, for instance. Such actions bring self-approval or a good conscience, if you will. Or they may act because of such strong passions as sensual and material needs, love, fear, or the quest for power. Both sets of actions frequently create disharmony with others; individuals foregoing the approval of others are often thought to be fools, bores, cranks, troublemakers, or misfits. In such instances, men are not usually concerned with "impression management."

For the most part, however, I think that Goffman is correct in his assessment of human interaction. While there are many motives that may guide men's behavior, I feel that man today (at least in American society) acts less because of convictions concerning what he thinks is right or wrong, or because of other intrinsic or extrinsic rewards, than because of a desire to be approved, loved, or accepted. This withering away of inner standards, this embracement of a market mentality and other-directedness, reflects—in my opinion—a general decline of moral standards in contemporary society. Thus, like Goffman, I see men coming together and presenting their best faces in an attempt to win recognition and approval from one another. This is man not as I wish him to be but, rather, as I find him today.

It might appear that thus far in the chapter my discussion has taken us far astray from the three questions with which I concluded the previous chapter: (1) Do the same social processes operate in data-collection activities as in other everyday social activities? (2) If so, why is it that people frequently emit "socially desirable" behavior in their interactions with others? and (3) What are the various elements that people consider as a basis for the direction and content of social interaction? To the first question, I offer my view that the *same* processes operate in the data-collection activity as operate in everyday conduct. An attempt to document this will constitute much of the remainder of this chapter, and the following chapter as well. Hopefully, at least a partial answer to the second question has been offered; people try to present favorable self-descriptions in social encounters because of their desire to receive the social approval of those with whom they interact. Let us now consider the last of the three questions above.

Ultimately my concern is with people's behavior in those data-collection activities in which the investigator and the subject of study encounter one another, but perhaps we can learn something about this by considering what occurs when two people come together in everyday situations. We know that in order for interaction in the fullest sense to take place there must be communication between the actors in the social situation. Each actor infers from the behavior of the other what idea or feelings or message the other is trying to convoy. Both individuals seek to acquire information about one another or to utilize information which they already possess. Individuals require this information about other actors in order to help them define the situation, so that they know what is expected from them and what they can expect from others. This means, of course, that in responding to others we all depend upon certain clues or cues which serve (a) to assist us in determining people's intentions and feelings, (b) to allow us to make certain judgments about the character of the persons themselves and what they expect from us, and (c) to facilitate communication. These clues or cues include, among other things, the settings in which people encounter one another, various physical and social attributes of the actors, nonverbal sources of communication, and the actors' utterances and vocal characteristics.[2]

Physical and Social Space

Consider, first, the physical settings in which people encounter one another. To take an obvious example, it makes an enormous difference whether we are asked for a light by a stranger in the midst of a busy supermarket during the daytime or at a deserted streetcorner late at night. The same behavior—requesting a light—will evoke very different definitions of the situation in the two instances. In the first, we most likely would see it merely as a request for a match needed to light a cigarette. In the second,

---

[2] Much in the remainder of this chapter is drawn from Barnlund's (1968) excellent book.

however, we might very well ask ourselves whether it is really only a match he is after or whether he might want something else: to rob us, physically assault us, or (if we are females) attack us sexually. Or to take another example, it makes a great difference whether a young man is introduced to his blind date at a church social or in a bar.

But it is not only *where* one meets someone that is significant, but also the physical surroundings. We saw in the previous chapter how beautiful and ugly rooms affect people's perceptions and motivation. It also seems likely that such things as colors, temperature, and noise level affect people's definitions of the situation and their subsequent behavior. The architect Saarinen (1948:128) has observed that people seldom fail to respond, in one way or another, upon entering a room, stating that "the influence of the room is stronger than our character. And our character is improved or depraved depending on whether the room is esthetically . . . on a higher or lower level than we ourselves." Unfortunately, however, very little is known about man's esthetic needs, or the effects of physical surroundings on people's behavior. Yet we have all probably had the experience of interacting with other persons in a room that seemed cold and sterile, and having our interaction affected by this. Crowded and dirty surroundings, as well, may affect the conduct of interpersonal relations (Jacobs, 1961).

In addition to the possible effects of physical space and surroundings on the content and direction of interactions, there is the influence of *personal* space and position. The literature contains several concepts relating to the matter of space and position. There is, first of all, the notion of territory as described by such writers as Whyte (1955) and Suttles (1968) to refer to some delimited physical area to which persons are psychologically attached and about which they exhibit proprietary attitudes. Another concept used to refer to an interactional area is that of region as used by Goffman (1959) to refer to some area of interaction which is bounded by barriers to perception. Sometimes these barriers are physical as in the case of fences between the houses in Park Forest described by Whyte (1956). Other physical barriers such as yards and streets may also control the interpersonal contacts and communication which people have with one another (Jacobs, 1961).

These physical barriers to communication such as territories, fences, streets, yards, restaurant counters, and those barriers which separate "front and back stage" regions (Goffman, 1959), are all usually stationary. But there is also a kind of boundary which we carry around with us as part of our person. This invisible boundary marks the limits beyond which we do not wish people to intrude when they interact with us. This sense of *personal* space differs, of course, among individuals and for various cultures. In discussing "how space communicates," Hall (1969a:162) observes that "not only is a vocal message qualified by the handling of distance, but the substance of a conversation can often demand special handling of space. There are certain things that are difficult to talk about unless one is within the proper conversational zone."

Hall goes on to note (Hall, 1969a:163–164) that various shifts in the voice are associated with specific ranges of distance in different cultures. When Americans stand "very close" to one another (3 to 6 inches apart) during a conversation it is usually when some secret is being conveyed, and it is expected that the conveyor of the message will speak in a soft whisper. When people converse at a "neutral" distance of some 20 to 30 inches, as they do when discussing some personal subject matter, they ordinarily speak in a soft voice. And when people stand at what Hall terms a "public distance" (5½ to 8 feet apart), it is usually when they have public information for others to hear. In this case, it is expected that they will speak in a somewhat loud, full voice. The manner in which verbal communication takes place is, it seems clear, partially dependent on people observing these rules of personal space. An encounter that begins with one individual speaking in a soft voice from a distance of 3 inches is likely to proceed differently from one that begins with an individual speaking in a loud voice from 3 inches away. And a conversation which begins with one person whispering softly to someone who is several feet away will probably take a different turn from one where a fuller, more audible, voice is used at the same distance. Both the individual who conveys private information in a loud voice across a crowded room and the one who approaches to within a few inches of the listener to convey what is normally thought of as public information for others to hear, are likely to be considered rude or odd by other persons in their presence, and subsequent definitions of the situation will be affected by these deviations from the norms regarding the rules of personal communication.

Another source of data concerning the significance of personal space is derived from studies of seating patterns. Steinzor (1950) found that individuals who are seated opposite one another in a discussion consistently interacted more than those seated next to one another. Sommer (1959, 1962, 1969) reports that people will choose to sit on couches opposite each other until the distance between the couches exceeds three and a half feet, at which point they prefer to sit next to one another on the same couch.

One study by Sommer (1965) shows that college students choose seats in accordance with the type of relationships which they anticipate with others. When casual and cooperative relations are expected, they choose close or corner positions at a rectangular table, while they select opposite or distant seating when competition is anticipated. Sommer (1965:346) notes that:

> These results indicate that different tasks are associated with different spatial arrangements; the ecology of interaction differs from the ecology of co-action and competition. Exactly why these particular arrangements are chosen we do not know for certain. On the basis of what our subjects report, eye contact seems an important factor in spatial arrangements. Under certain conditions direct visual contact represents a challenge to the other, a play at dominance.

To any male who has ridden the New York subways, Sommer's findings strike a familiar note. With long benches facing one another one each side of the subway car, the best position from which to view an attractive female is not next to her (where observation involves the turning of one's body to observe her profile) nor directly across from her (where one's stares are not easily hidden and where it is difficult to avoid eye contact). Rather the best position is a seat at an angle across the aisle from her, where observation is possible without acrobatics or risk of detection. That detection is likely was shown by evidence presented by Gibson and Pick (1963) who found that people know with a high degree of certainty when someone is looking them full in the face. If one were interested not so much in an undisclosed observation as in making the acquaintance of a female subway traveler, then a seat directly across from her would probably be preferable, as it would maximize opportunities for eye contact, smiling gestures, or whatever behaviors our man-in-the-subway deems most appropriate for accomplishing his mission.

A further indication of what seating arrangements convey can be seen if we consider someone entering a subway, bus, or train in which only a few seats are taken. An individual who selects a seat directly next to someone on any of these forms of transportation or sits directly across from an already seated person on a subway places himself in a position where his "strange" behavior threatens other people.

Physical and Social Attributes

Although interpersonal communications are affected by environmental qualities, physical settings, and personal space, these are undoubtedly less important than the various physical and social attributes of the interactors. These physical and social attributes constitute, in Goffman's terms (1959:2) the expressions that an individual *gives off*. They are, according to Goffman, one of the two types of sign activity on the part of the interacting individual, the other being the expressions that a person gives: words and gestures. Taken together, signs given and given-off help to define the situation for the interactors. In the words of Barnlund (1968:518), "Studies of how social judgments are formed suggest that appraisals of others are made effortlessly and with little conscious awareness. In a few seconds, the perceiver gains enough information from a visual inspection of posture, face, hands, and clothing to form a clear image of the other person and to guide his own responses to him."

In any social encounter, it seems likely that the most obvious and readily apparent bases for social judgment are the social and physical attributes of the actors. Such social attributes as sex, age, race, and sometimes ethnicity, are visible to other actors and are not easily hidden. Physical attributes such as height, weight, and the various qualities that constitute physical appearance are also rather apparent to the interactors, although these may more easily be altered in various ways: with girdles, lifts in the shoes, falsies, face creams, and the like.

Clearly, sex and race are two attributes which are virtually always noticed by persons who come together, and both of these attributes influence people's definitions of the situation. Another attribute which is visible to people who encounter one another is their age, although age is a quality that is apt to be given somewhat less attention by actors than sex and race. Not only is it less salient for most interactions, but it is also less visible. People can do a good deal to hide and alter their appearance with regard to age, and often one can only estimate that someone is in his late 30's or early 40's.

Every individual brings with him to all social encounters certain recognitions and expectations about what he can anticipate from people with certain attributes and what they can expect from him. As a result of the socialization process, he has learned the social significance of male and female, Negro and white, young and old. The social distinctions indicated by these attributes operate to define the context in which communication occurs.

Not all social attributes, however, are as readily apparent as sex, age, and race. Such attributes as marital status, education, occupation, and social class, for example, must be determined or disclosed through various cues and probes. Wedding rings, modes of dress, and accents may be signs given-off. Signs are given by such things as a woman's utterance, "If only my husband could be here today," or by a male's casual remark that, "I had a chair like this when I was at Harvard," or by someone's assertion that, "We've had the same problem with our summer cottage in France." Or the individual who desires to find out something of the non-visible attributes of someone else may ask: "Does your wife like it here?" Or the question might be asked, "Did you read it when you were in college?" Or, perhaps, "Where do you live?" All of these constitute certain cues or probes designed either to disclose or to discover certain information about people's attributes.

Another set of attributes which play a large part in most social interactions concerns people's physical appearance, including their height, weight, facial characteristics, posture, physical mannerisms, and grooming. These not only provide cues as to what we can expect from others and they from us, but also serve as a basis for judgments about other persons.

Both an individual's height and his weight are involved in people's assessments of his character, his desirability as an acquaintance, and his general worth as a human being. In American society, heavy stress is placed on the importance of physical attractiveness. Efforts expended in pursuit of having an attractive body are truly colossal. One of the factors that most seriously detracts from bodily attractiveness in our society is being overweight; fatness is evaluated negatively as unesthetic and as an indication of self-indulgence and lack of willpower. Fashion models and movie actresses are seldom overweight, much less fat. Nor are other culture heroes, such as athletes and male television and movie personalities, likely to be fat. People who are fat find themselves evaluated in terms of a general cultural value emphasizing thinness.

Several recent studies have been concerned with public reactions toward obesity in American society. Richardson and his associates (1961; Goodmen et al., 1963) have investigated cultural uniformities in reaction to various physical disabilities. Both adults and children were presented with six black and white line drawings depicting a "normal" child, a child with a brace on the leg and with crutches, a child sitting in a wheel chair with a blanket over both legs, a child with his left hand missing, a child with facial disfigurement on one side of the mouth, and a grossly overweight child. Individuals were asked to rank the pictures in terms of the likability of persons like those depicted. Consistently, the overweight child was ranked as least likable. This conclusion was true regardless of the evaluator's sex, age, race, rural-urban residence, socioeconomic status, or their own disabilities. A similar study by Maddox et al. (1968:297) concludes that "in five samples . . . of adults selected from populations reasonably expected to have different attitudes toward fatness, indications of a negative stereotype of fatness were consistently and pervasively found." Thus, both of these investigations appear to reflect negative views of fat persons in our society. It may also be the case, of course, that people who are grossly underweight are subject to negative evaluations by others. However, in a society like our own, it is rather unlikely that extreme problems of underweight will be very prevalent.

Not only people's weight, but their height as well, enters into their assessments of one another, and their subsequent behavior. In American society, men can, in a sense, be stigmatized by a lack of height and women by an excess of height. A common everyday instance in which height clearly makes a considerable difference can be seen in American dating and marriage patterns. Since men are generally taller than women, it is expected that with dates and mates, as well, men should be taller. A couple in which the wife is 2 inches taller than her spouse will draw far more stares and comment than one where the husband is 6 or 8 inches taller than his wife. That many men feel awkward and ill at ease in the presence of a taller woman can be seen by the various devices which men employ to minimize these differences in height: trying to escape standing close to a taller woman so as to avoid ease of comparison; leaning against something or slightly slouching, thus giving the impression that if he really wanted to stand tall and straight he would be taller than the female; attempting to steer her to a place where they both can be seated so that her height superiority will not be noticed. And, of course, the tall woman will herself frequently feel ill at ease with her excessive height, as can be witnessed in the hunching of shoulders and bowing of the head characteristic of many tall women. As we can see from the above examples, physical size is indeed a factor which people consider in their relationships with others.

It is also interesting to consider not only the effects of size, but of posture as well. An early study that considered the possible influence of posture was conducted by James (1932) who photographed almost 350 different arrangements of a human manikin with the hope of discovering whether postures were considered expressive of certain emotions. He found that various positions were interpreted as symptomatic of inner states and that certain postures were viewed as giving general clues to people's attitudes. James (1932:426) notes that,

the posture as a whole is an ensemble or constellation of different parts. Of these, the head and trunk are . . . the most significant for the specification of the posture. The distribution of the weight of the body, the expansion or contraction of the chest, the raised or dropped shoulders are other factors which, each in its own setting, are important. Every one of these has in any particular position its own expression.

A similar observation is offered by Lowen (1958:87) who says:

because we express our personalities or character in every action and in every attitude it booomes possible to determine character traits from such diverse expressions as handwriting, the walk of the person, etc., , , , Most important, however, is the physical appearance at rest and in movement. No words are so clear as the language of body expression once one has learned to read it.

An example of the manner in which the body appears to convey certain aspects of a people's personality is provided by Susan Sontag, who speaks of the "coolness" and "stiffness" of Swedes in Stockholm as follows (Sontag, 1969:30–31): "It's true that the Swedes are spectacularly good-looking, but a discrepancy between beauty of face and unliberated body is fairly common. The inhibition is less apparent in the body at rest than in its pattern of movement: little mobility of the head; inexpressive shoulders; locked pelvis; inflexible, too erect carriage." In summary, then, it appears that the manner in which a person holds his body indicates his mood, perhaps his background, and his present accessibility to human interchange.

Although people respond to certain cues associated with different physiques and different postures, as well as to a person's physique or posture itself, no aspect of a man's appearance is as important in providing both expressive cues and a basis for social judgments as his face. Not only do we make evaluations about people's attitudes and feelings (sad, happy, pensive, aloof, etc.) from their facial expressions but, perhaps equally important, we make judgments as to their attractiveness. intentions, and approachability on the basis of facial characteristics.

This is especially the case in the United States where so much emphasis is placed on the importance of good looks: a clear complexion, white evenly spaced teeth, a narrow aquiline nose, small ears set close to the head, and whatever other, often unspecified, features make an individual handsome, attractive, pretty, or good-looking. The individual who falls short of these standards to such an extent that he is considered ugly, unattractive, or nondescript often suffers more than merely a negative description of his facial features. For people whom others judge as unattractive are also frequently seen as inferior in other ways; their facial limitations are viewed as evidence of their general lack of moral and spiritual worth, of their unworthiness as human beings with whom others would want to associate. This appears to be especially the case for women in our society.

Obviously there are no completely agreed upon standards of facial beauty, even within a single culture. But there is probably greater agreement as to what constitutes *undesirable* facial features, at least in American society. Acne, even though a phenomenon experienced by many teenagers, is a blemish which detracts from an individual's facial appearance, as do pockmarks, scars, large pores, moles, warts, freckles, facial hair among women, squinty eyes, thyroid or bulging eyes, excessively large noses, wide nostrils, cauliflower ears, elephant ears, thick lips, thin lips, buck teeth, yellow or discolored teeth, very small (weak) chins, overly prominent jaws, unusually short or long necks, as well as various deficiencies concerning the length, thickness, texture, amount, or even color of a person's hair. These constitute only a partial listing of the facial features which people are confronted with when meeting another person. If our encounter with another is sufficiently fleeting and superficial, we may pay no particular attention to his facial characteristics. Or in a firmly established relationship we may no longer notice certain aspects of someone's facial features, though the relation may have been formed either in spite of or because of these features. But in most instances where we meet someone and are in his presence for more than a few minutes we pay a good deal of attention to his facial appearance. We do not always, or perhaps even usually, focus on his features individually, but rather on the general *gestalt* of his face. This means that oftentimes, for example, we can remember that a woman was very attractive without being able to describe her individual facial features in other than a very vague manner.

It is, of course, not surprising that the face should be given so much attention in our interactions with others. All conversations are marked by mutual glances between the speakers; one frequently looks or stares at the other while he speaks, as well as occasionally glancing at him to determine that he is listening to what we are saying. This means that, at least in the initial stages of our acquaintanceship with another, we will spend a good deal of time observing his face. Whether we will want to meet him again, the kind of relationship we envision with him, and our general feelings about him, are all determined to some extent by our assessment of his facial attractiveness and our judgments of the relation of his facial features to his general character or attractiveness as someone for us to know.

But we observe the face of others not only as a means of forming judgments about their attractiveness, we also view the face as a means for acquiring cues as to people's underlying feelings and emotions. Barnlund (1968:521) puts it very well when he states:

> Of all the features that identify a man, none is as differentiating as his face; of all the parts of the body, none is as richly expressive. By means of a complex masculature, facial surfaces may be maneuvered in many ways, supplying constant if rapidly changing evidence of inner states. The face may reflect what is being experienced, may obscure it, or may falsify it, though dissembling facially may be more difficult than it is verbally. The impulse to get a better view of a speaker, whether in a conversation or the theatre, seldom arises from inability to see his feet, shoulders, hips, or trunk, but from fear of losing an essential part of the message because qualifying facial cues are hidden.

The face, then, serves as an enormously important source for expressions given-off. The seemingly cool and sophisticated individual who begins to perspire profusely, or blushes, or who develops a facial tic during an argument may find these signs interpreted as evidence that he is far less cool and sophisticated than he pretends to be; the person who nods and grunts as he listens to our talking but at the same time constantly directs his eyes to others, gives evidence of being less interested and engrossed in what we are saying than he would like us to believe; the man who responds to a telephone request to attend a party by saying that he would be delighted but at the same time has a long face for those in his presence, is telling us (though not the telephoner) that he is actually less than delighted at the party invitation.

Nonverbal Communication

Empirical evidence for the communication of nonverbal behavior can be seen in studies by Eckman (1964), in which photographs and written speech samples of interviewing sessions were to be correlated by a group of judges. Each judge had the speech samples along with pairs of photographs from which they were asked to select the one from each pair that they thought accompanied the speech sample. In one of the experiments (Eckman, 1964), in which the "whole person was presented in the photographs, more than three-quarters of the judges scored above the expected median—thus indicating a strong relationship between body and head position and verbal behavior." Another one of Eckman's (1964) experiments showed that judges were much more accurate in relating verbal to nonverbal behavior when they had the whole person to judge than when they had only the body position with the head excluded from the photographs. In still another experiment, Eckman (1964) found that a group of judges responding only to head cues achieved greater accuracy in matching photographs to verbal behavior than a group seeing only body position cues. Eckman concludes from these experiments that "some information related to the verbal behavior is conveyed by spontaneous non-verbal behavior during interviews."

Another aspect of one's physical behavior that was mentioned earlier concerns the eye contact and glances at others that are involved in nonverbal communication. The importance of the eyes was noted by Simmel (1921:358) when he said: "By the same act in which the observer seeks to know the observed, he surrenders himself to be understood. . . . The eye cannot take unless at the same time it gives." And Lowen (1958:93) states that, "It must be with some reason that the eyes are regarded as the mirrors of the soul. . . . Some eyes are bright and sparkle, some shine like stars, others are dull and may be vacant. . . . Some eyes are sad, others are angry; some are cold and hard, others are soft and appealing."

Apparently, an individual engaged in conversation with another person looks more at the other when that person is speaking than when he himself is speaking. Nielson (1962) reports this finding for a group of Harvard students when they were engaged in heated discussion. And a study by Exline et al. (1965) found that individuals in a laboratory situation looked more at the investigator when listening than when speaking to him or her. They found in the same investigation that people looked less often at the person with whom they were interacting when personal matters were being discussed than when the discussion was about more general matters. In discussing the exchange and avoidance of mutual glances, the investigators (Exline et al., 1965:201) observe that

> in general a continued exchange of glances would seem to signal a willingness or a desire to become involved with one another, or to maintain an ongoing interaction. Avoidance, on the other hand, would seem to indicate a lack of interest in initiating a relationship, or in the case of an ongoing interaction, would indicate that one or both parties wished to break away. If, for example, one wished to avoid receiving or sending signs of effective arousal one might act to accomplish these ends by avoiding eye contact with the others.

In a previous study, Exline (1963) had found mutual glances to be more prevalent between women than between men. The later investigation (Exline et al., 1965) found that females showed more overall eye contact with the investigator, regardless of that person's sex. The authors suggest that these sex differences in eye contact result from women's greater orientation toward affectionate and inclusive relationships with others. Whatever the reasons for greater eye contact among women, it seems clear that men and women alike will sometimes indicate a desire to maintain psychological distance from other persons by avoiding eye contact with them.

Avoidance of eye contact is, of course, a familiar device that we all use in our everyday activities. Spying someone whom we wish to avoid, we stare past him, over his head, to the right or left, keep our eyes down, or let our eyes cloud over as if we are in deep thought and unable to see his attempts to catch our eye. Or we indicate our desire to terminate a conversation by staring at other objects or people in the vicinity, both while speaking to someone and while, ostensibly, listening. These signs given-off may refute our verbal assertions that we wish to continue the conversation.

While the face and eyes are the focal points for most inter-action, the hands, and even the feet, give off certain signals. The drumming, tapping, and interlacing of fingers, fidgeting with one's hands with a cigarette, rubbing one's hands together, wiping one's hands, trembling, scratching, clapping the hands together, snapping the fingers, placing one's head in his hands, cracking the knuckles, pounding with the fists, the clenching of fists, the slapping of one's forehead, and the placing of a finger on the lips are all movements that people frequently make. That hand movements are capable of communication is shown by two early experiments by Carmichael (1937). In these investigations, an actor was seated behind a curtain so that only his hands were visible. He was instructed to use his hands to portray several emotions. People who were shown photographs of these hand gestures agreed substantially on what emotions were being conveyed. When the emotions were portrayed in motion pictures there was somewhat greater agreement among people than when still pictures were used. The feet too convey various feeling states through tapping, shaking, shuffling, etc. Through the hands and feet people give-off signs concerning nervousness, surprise, anger, fear, attentiveness, and other emotions.

The extent to which the use of hand gestures varies among different cultural groups is shown in a study cited by Barnlund (1968:531) in which Efron (1941) found sharp contrasts in the gestures used by Jewish and Italian immigrants: "Eastern European Jews tended to use gestures of smaller radius executed close to the upper part of the body and angular and jerky in movement, while Southern Italians used movements of greater radius sweeping from head to knees and involving the whole body. These gestural dialects generally disappeared as the groups were assimilated into American life." A more recent book by Ruesch and Kees (1956:22) speaks of the meaning of gestures in several different cultures: "Gesture among the Americans is largely oriented toward activity; among the Italians it serves the purpose of illustration and display; among the Jews it is a device of emphasis; among the Germans it specifies both attitude and commitment; and among the French it is an expression of style and containment."

Vocal Behavior

One aspect of vocal behavior concerns the signs which people give-off. What they say is obviously an important determinant of how other persons define the situation, the kinds of judgments they make about one another, and the direction of subsequent inter-action. If, for instance, someone we meet for the first time says, "I have been dying to meet you," our expectations as to what we can anticipate from him and he from us are very much different than if he acknowledges the introduction with a remark like, "I'd hoped that I could avoid having to meet you." Similarly, whether people tell us we are bright or stupid, handsome or ugly, honest or dis-honest, conveys a great deal as to what their feelings are about us.

But it is not only the content of what people say to one another that is involved in what they communicate to one another and the mutual judgments they make, for there are various vocal character-istics which are involved in communication: the volume of people's voices, voice qualities, speech cadence, and inflectional patterns.[3]

[3] A good example of the different meanings conveyed by one or another emphasis or inflection is provided by Rosten (1970:xvi) who states that with Yiddish, "The same sentence may be put through maneuvers of matchless versatility: (1) *Two* tickets for her concert I should buy? (Meaning: 'I'm having enough trouble deciding if it's worth one.'); (2) Two *tickets* for her concert I should buy? ('You mean to say she isn't distributing free passes? The hall will be empty!'); (3) Two tickets for *her* concert I should buy? ('Did she buy tickets to *my* daughter's recital?'); (4) Two tickets for her *concert* I should buy? ('You mean to say they call what she does a "concert"?'); (5) Two tickets for her concert *I* should buy? ('After what she did to me?'); (6) Two tickets for her concert I *should* buy? ('Are you giving me lessons in ethics?'); (7) Two tickets for her concert I should *buy*? ('I wouldn't go even if she gave me a complimentary!')."

Frequently, for instance, we try to locate people in terms of their regional or geographical backgrounds by listening to their accents, inflections, and rates of speech. Americans who speak of "*insurance*," for instance, often reveal themselves as being from either a border state or from the South. Depending on our views of the South and its people, our subsequent interaction with an individual whom we locate in this manner may be more or less positive than if we had located him as being from New York or from Maine. An individual who through the rather precise and mincing manner of speaking adopted by some male homosexuals is defined by us as a "fag" may be reacted to much differently than a person without these vocal characteristics.

Not only do we make judgments about where people are from, the kinds of people they are, and what can be expected from them on the basis of their vocal characteristics, but we also make judgments about their moods and how they feel. Several studies have focused on examining the relationship between various emotions and different vocal patterns. Fairbanks and Pronovost (1939) had actors use the same paragraph to convey such emotions as grief, anger, and fear, finding that emotions expressed by voice alone were readily identifiable. Another study by Davitz and Davitz (1959) had subjects recite parts of the alphabet to convey feelings of anger, fear, happiness, jealousy, love, nervousness, pride, sadness, satisfaction, and sympathy. Judges were given the task of identifying tape recordings of the various feelings expressed through the reading of the alphabet. For all ten emotions, the judges showed a surprising ability to correctly identify the emotions expressed. There were, however, some differences in the extent to which they made correct identifications; anger and nervousness were most readily identified, while pride and jealousy were least readily given a correct identification. Reviewing the literature concerned with vocal expressions of emotion, Davitz (1964:23) concludes that: "regardless of the techniques used, all studies of adults thus far reported in the literature agree that emotional meanings can be communicated accurately by vocal expression." Again these empirical findings correspond to our own everyday observations that people are depressed or unhappy—observations based not so much on *what* people say as on *how* they say it.

We have seen, then, that each of us depends on a number of "sign vehicles," as Goffman (1959:1) calls them, in making judgments about what we can expect of other people and what they can expect from us. Unfortunately, most social research has been concerned with the expressions which people give in conveying information rather than with the expressions given-off. That is, the focus has been on verbal rather than nonverbal communication. As we have seen in our brief review, however, all of us communicate nonverbally. We raise an eyebrow or gesture with a hand, meet someone's eyes and look away, shift our posture, rub our noses, and so on. While social scientists have only recently begun to collect systematic data on these nonverbal communications, the recent work of Goffman (1959, 1963, 1967), Hall (1959a, 1966b), and Birdwhistell (1952, 1960) should remind us of the vast complexities involved in studying human behavior.

Let me now review briefly the concerns of this chapter. I began by arguing that the process of collecting sociological data is itself a social process, having features in common with other situations of human interaction. Following this presentation, I presented some of my background assumptions concerning the nature of man and of human interaction, including my belief that the need for social approval is an important need which people bring with them to most social encounters. The final, and largest, portion of this chapter dealt with some of the elements or factors that people consider as a basis of information about others with whom they come into contact. In the chapter that follows, our attention will return to a consideration of some of these factors as they enter into data-collection activities where the investigator and the subjects of study encounter one another.

Chapter IV

Social Processes in Survey Research

I argued in Chapter I that much of what sociologists *know* about social behavior and interaction is a result of the behavior and interaction involved in the process of collecting their data. Hence, as was documented in Chapter II, the data which sociologists obtain in their research activities reflect the effects not only of the variables of principal research interest but of other factors in the situation as well. As I noted in the previous chapter, however, these situational factors can be considered from two viewpoints. To the researcher, the systematic effects of situational factors other than the objects of measurement constitute sources of bias and contamination in the measurement procedure. From a broader perspective, however, these so-called biases (sources of error) represent the content of everyday interaction. Or, as Friedman (167:xi) has so succinctly put it: "One man's error variance is another man's social behavior."

My attempt to show how these various factors (sex, age, social status, etc.) operate in everyday activities constituted the major part of the previous chapter. I presented my views of what happens when two people come together, stressing the manner in which they look for and respond to various sources of information about one another. In turning now to a consideration of what occurs when data collectors and the subjects of research interest confront one another, I shall focus my attention on the interaction that constitutes the relationship between the interviewer and the respondent in survey studies. While the processes in almost all data-collection activities by sociologists have much in common with other everyday social activities, the survey interview should be given especially close scrutiny because of its widespread use as the primary, and often sole, source of sociological data. Webb et al. (1966:1) have commented on the heavy use of interviews (and questionnaires) as follows:

> We lament this overdependence upon a single, fallible method. Interviews and questionnaires intrude as a foreign element into the social setting they would describe, they create as well as measure attitudes, they elicit atypical roles and responses, they are limited to those who are accessible and will cooperate, and the responses obtained are produced in part by dimensions of individual differences irrelevant to the topic at hand.

I, too, lament such overdependence on interviews and questionnaires. And, as will be seen in Chapter VI, I see considerable merit in their suggestions regarding multiple and unobtrusive measures. But lacking in Webb et al.'s consideration of interviews and questionnaires is a recognition that the processes which operate in data-collection activities employing these procedures (especially interviews) are the very same processes that operate in many other everyday human interactions. From the viewpoint of Webb et al., therefore, "the responses obtained are produced in part by dimensions of individual differences irrelevant to the topic at hand." From another viewpoint, however, the responses obtained are produced by dimensions of individual differences *relevant to all social encounters.*

From either perspective, it seems clear that we should look closely at those data-collection procedures which provide such a high proportion of the data on which sociological knowledge is based. Let me consider, then, the survey situation. In so doing, no attempt will be made to distinguish among a number of different types of interviews in that my discussions will be sufficiently general to apply to several different interview types. The point I will try to illustrate in this chapter is that both interviewers and respondents employ the same mechanisms in the survey interview situation that they employ in many other social situations. My attempt is partially to elaborate, in a somewhat speculative manner, on Cicourel's (1964:101) assertion that

> canons of research demand that the interviewer operate somewhat like a computer with all the appearances of a fellow human being, but, so far as we know, persons in everyday life find it impossible either to present themselves as both or to receive presentations of others (regardless of the form it takes) which conform to the strict canons of scientific inquiry.

Interviewers and respondents can no more avoid mechanisms which produce biases in data-collection activities than they can avoid them in other everyday social activities. We should not forget in our constant concern with extrapolating from the interview to the real or social world, that the interview is itself a part of that real and that social world (Friedman, 1967).

As when two people meet in other social situations, when the interviewer and the respondent encounter one another, they begin to talk, to respond to various social stimuli, with each inferring from the behavior of the other (whether speech, gestures, posture, or whatever) what ideas or feelings the other person is trying to convey. Goffman (1959:249) puts it this way:

> When one individual enters the presence of others, he will want to discover the facts of the situation. Were he to possess this information, he could know, and make allowances for, what will come to happen and he could give the others present as much of their due as is consistent with his enlightened self-interest. . . . Full information of this order is rarely available; in its absence, the individual tends to em-

ploy substitutes—cues, tests, hints, expressive gestures, status symbols, etc.—as predictive devices. In short, since the reality that the individual is concerned with is unpredictable at the moment, appearances must be relied upon in its stead.

Some of the substitutes which Goffman speaks of as "predictive devices" were considered at length in the previous chapter, including physical and social space; such social attributes as sex, race, and education; physical qualities like height, weight, facial appearance, and posture, and a variety of vocal characteristics. All of these doubtlessly operate in the interview situation as well. Only a few of them, however, will be considered here.

Consider what occurs when an interviewer and a respondent come together in a typical survey research situation. The average interviewer is most likely either a middle-aged housewife employed by a professional social science research institute, or a graduate student working for a social science institute or directly for a sociologist associated with a university. Depending on the sampling procedure utilized, the interviewer will usually have the responsibility of interviewing: (a) a specific individual chosen as part of a random sample, (b) any person meeting certain specifications and living within a designated residence, or (c) any person meeting certain specifications and living within a designated area. In the case of (a) above, the potential respondent may or may not know that he is to be interviewed. If he does know, he may have been informed by letter or by telephone, and a formal appointment might have been made. With (b) and (c) above, it is unlikely that a potential respondent has been warned in advance of the impending interview. It is probably most often the case, therefore, that an individual who is to be interviewed in a social survey does not know it until that time when he is informed of the fact by a stranger standing at his door.

We have, then, a situation in which two strangers confront one another, although they are not equally strange to one another. While the potential respondent has no prior information about the interviewer, the reverse is not true. The interviewer has had the opportunity of viewing the respondent's home, as well as the neighborhood in which it is situated. He may have some prior information as to the kinds of people who live in the area (professional persons or blue-collar workers, Italians or Negroes, for example). The interviewer is also able to assess such clues to the respondent's identity and character as are provided by a car in the driveway, toys in the yard, the condition of the house and grounds, a nameplate on the door, as well as what he is able to observe when the future respondent answers his knock at the door or ringing of the doorbell.

In addition to the information which the interviewer, perhaps only partially in a conscious manner, gathers before actually meeting the respondent, he also usually possesses some information as to the purpose of the proposed interview: to determine people's voting habits, sexual behavior, mental health status, attitudes toward various groups of people, opinions on various matters, or whatever. Sometimes, especially in those situations where the interviewer is a graduate student working for a sociologist on a research project, he may even know the exact hypotheses which are to be tested through the data accumulated.

In any case, the interviewer almost always knows more about the potential respondent than the respondent knows about him. When the person selected for interview answers the door, he is confronted with an individual carrying one or another "behavior-objects," as Barnlund (1968:153) calls them: a briefcase, large envelope, or clipboard that helps announce the theme of the encounter. Frequently, the theme announced is one in which the respondent anticipates an attempt on the part of the stranger to sell him something. In anticipation of this eventuality and to eliminate the potential respondent's reluctance to admit him into the house, the interviewer is usually equipped with a pitch—similar to the pitch used by many salesmen. The purpose of such a pitch is to introduce himself and to say something about the sponsorship of the study (Gordon, 1969). Often, it goes something like this: "Good morning, I'm Mrs. Jones from ——— (Big Top University, the Social Science Research Institute). We are conducting a survey here in ——— to try to find out how people feel about a number of things (issues, questions, problems). I wonder if I might take a few minutes of your time to speak with you?" To this, the potential respondent may

answer affirmatively or he may exhibit skepticism about the interviewer's purposes. At this time, the interviewer may show him written credentials, which state that: "Mrs. Jones is on the staff of the
Social Science Research Institute, and is involved in gathering
information from a number of persons selected for interviewing.
Your cooperation in this scientific study will be most appreciated.
Sincerely, T. P. Lazerton, Ph.D., Study Director."

Assuming that the interviewer has gained entry to the premises,
he will then (either in response to the other's inquiries or as part of
his spiel) explain something about the purpose of the interview, and
will usually also explain how and why a particular respondent was
chosen. Sometimes the interviewer will assure the respondent that
he is "just a number" and that what he has to say will be kept completely confidential. The respondent is further informed of the
great importance of honest and frank answers or, when appropriate to the content of the interview schedule, he is told that there
are no right or wrong answers. In doing all of this, the interviewer
has the task of appearing friendly, so as to establish rapport with
the respondent. It should be emphasized, of course, that the interview is not really a conversation in the usual sense. The two
interactors are not free to choose topics or to range widely in their
discussions (Denzin, 1970). Rather, both the topics for discussion
and the range of such discussions are usually determined entirely
by the interviewer.

Prior to the actual start of the interview, the respondent and the
interviewer are both involved to some extent in sizing up one
another. This is especially the case for the prospective respondent
who asks himself a number of questions: I wonder how they really
picked me for this? What are they trying to find out? What will
happen if I give the wrong answers? Can I be honest with this
person if I am asked personal questions? To assist himself in
answering these questions, the respondent will give careful scrutiny
to various interviewer characteristics: sex, age, race, physical appearance, accent, and whatever other qualities people consider in
their face-to-face encounters with other persons. As the interview
proceeds, the respondent may search for certain signs given-off
that may reveal something about the way that the interviewer himself feels about various responses. At the same time, the interviewer

is engaged in a similar appraisal of the signs given-off by the respondent. He must ascertain: Does he trust me? Does he think I am friendly? Will he give honest answers? In addition, the interviewer must sometimes pay attention to certain clues signifying the identity or character of the respondent—for example, such things as the room in which the interview is being conducted, including its contents: books, magazines, cigarettes, empty glasses, or whatever.

In a very real sense, both the interviewer and the respondent utilize various methodological skills in their encounter with one another. The interviewer searches for indicators that will reveal the respondent's true feelings on matters relating to the content of the interview schedule, as well as to the respondent's true feelings about the interviewer and the interview situation. Some of these indicators are, of course, contained within the interview schedule itself. Others are the signs given-off by the respondent, some of which the interviewer has been trained as *interviewer* to be sensitive to, some of which the interviewer responds to as a natural part of everyday conduct. Gordon (1969:67) in his discussion of interviewing strategy lists the interviewer's responsibilities with regard to nonverbal elements as follows:

> for maximal utilization of non-verbal respondent-to-interviewer communication, the interviewer's tasks are: a) to observe a broad range of non-verbal activity and be alert for inconsistencies; b) to be alert for *changes* in the respondent's non-verbal activity. . . ; and c) to interpret the meaning of any inconsistencies and changes in non-verbal behavior in the broader context of the verbal communication and the situation in which the interview is taking place.

Although not programmed for the task in the same manner, the respondent also considers signs given and given-off—although he is concerned with other matters including, mainly, some estimate as to what the interviewer expects of him, and some hints or clues as to how the interviewer will evaluate, judge, and utilize the responses which he gives to the interviewer's inquiries. The principal difference between the objectives of the two participants in the interview situation is that the interviewer's chief goal is to obtain the best (most valid) data possible from the respondent, while the respondent's chief concern is with obtaining the interviewer's social approval, or at least avoiding his disapproval.

As Rosenberg (1965, 1969) has shown for laboratory experiments, subjects in social science investigations spend a good deal of time hypothesizing about the kinds of responses that will win approval. Rosenberg (1969:3) states:

> The particular difficulty with the state of affairs is that subjects in groups experiencing comparatively high levels of evaluation apprehension will be more prone than subjects in other groups to interpret the experimenter's instructions, explanations, and measures for what this may convey about the kinds of responses that will be considered healthy or unhealthy, mature or immature. In other words, they will develop hypotheses about how to win positive evaluation or to avoid negative evaluation.

Rosenberg (1969:74) goes on to suggest that:

> More often than not, [the subject] will speculatively examine the instructions he has received, the overall rationale that has been provided, the procedures and measuring devices to which he has been exposed; and out of the questions these raise for him and the hints they convey to him he will, if at all possible, draw some meaning, some guiding hypothesis about what is really being investigated and how he can best display himself to the investigator.

While all persons try to present themselves in a good light, people obviously differ in the strength of their need to be thought well of by others. The implications of this are clearly stated by Crowne and Marlowe (1964:27):

> for those whose need is high, we could assume a generalized expectancy that approval satisfactions are attained by engaging in behaviors which are culturally sanctioned and

approved. . . . [It] is simply not considered desirable in the contemporary social milieu to indicate on a test that one is anxious. frustrated, unhappy. and beset by all sorts of strange thoughts and impulses.

Not only do people differ in their need for social approval, but they also differ in the ways they perceive, evaluate, and respond to the cues present in any social situation. That is, while all persons concern themselves with what Goffman calls "the facts of the situation," not all persons judge the facts in the same way. But when a group of persons whom one is interested in comparing with other groups judges the facts in a systematic manner, it often results in what the researcher regards as a systematic bias. Responses to an interviewer's questions seem especially susceptible to purposeful distortion by someone with a strong need for social approval, in that such an individual is sensitive to saying the right thing. The purpose of the questions is frequently obvious to the respondent; the implications of his answers may be apparent to him; and he can consciously control his responses—the signs given. This means, as Cook and Selltiz (1964:40) note, that "a person who wishes to give a certain picture of himself—whether in order to impress the tester favorably, to preserve his own self-image, or for some other reason—can rather easily do so." This problem of the "social desirability effect" was considered at some length in Chapter II, where the studies of Clark and Tifft (1966), Dohrenwend (1966), and Phillips and Clancy (1970) were discussed. Since, at least among middle-class Americans, the most desirable responses are those that define one as happy, healthy, rational, unprejudiced, well adjusted, and democratic, it is likely that a good deal of distortion will be found in some people's responses to questions concerning these matters. Knowing this, social scientists have developed a number of procedures to make it easier for respondents to admit to undesirable qualities, feelings, and experience. A list of these procedures is offered by Cook and Selltiz (1964:41–42): (1) assurances of anonymity; (2) emphasizing that there are no right or wrong answers; (3) stating that people differ in their views of these things; (4) stressing the importance of honest answers in order to contribute to scientific knowledge; (5) increasing rapport so as to create the impression that the investigator will not disapprove of any answer; (6) including items to which an unfavorable reply is likely to be considered acceptable; (7) wording items in such a way that they assume that the subject holds certain attitudes or views (such as, "When did you first become angry with the person?").

All of the above procedures are designed to increase the validity of our measuring instruments. Recall that measures may be invalidated by showing that they correlate highly with some conceptually simpler variable, such as the tendency to respond in a socially desirable manner to all items. Thus, if the relationship of social desirability to an investigator's chief independent and dependent variables can be determined, the discriminant validity of his measures may be increased. As was mentioned earlier in this report, psychologists frequently obtain estimates of item desirability as part of the data which they collect from their subjects. Sociologists, however, almost never obtain such estimates, even though the existence of social desirability effects is implicitly recognized in the utilization of such procedures as assuring anonymity and emphasizing the importance of honest answers.

It is, in fact, surprising that sociologists usually fail to obtain measures of social desirability in their studies, especially when we consider their great concern with social norms. If, as is so often the case with sociological explanations, it is assumed that people conform to the norms of the groups to which they belong, then it should be expected that the same mechanisms will operate in the interview situation. Although there is little empirical evidence concerning this question, I suspect that many of the findings of sociological investigators can be interpreted in terms of certain norms held in common by middle-class interviewers and respondents.

Consider, for instance, studies of happiness, mental illness, and racial prejudice. Consistently such investigations have revealed greater happiness (Bradburn and Caplovitz, 1965; Phillips, 1965), better mental health (Dohrenwend, 1966; Srole et al., 1962), and less racial prejudice among middle-class persons than among people from lower social strata. It may be that the results of these studies do, indeed, represent true differences among the various social classes. But an alternative possibility is that middle-class

persons are more aware than lower-class ones as to what interviewers consider the most socially desirable responses to questions
concerning happiness, mental illness, and racial prejudice. For
middle-class persons have probably learned that they are supposed
to be happy, well adjusted, and free of negative attitudes toward
various racial and ethnic groups. If these middle-class individuals
are interviewed by middle-class interviewers, as is usually the case,
they may be reluctant to admit to certain undesirable characteristics
or feelings. That is, they may be unwilling to incur the interviewers'
disapproval by giving what are, for middle-class persons, undesirable responses. Among people from lower strata, on the other
hand, there may be less reluctance to be frank and honest about
their true feelings in that they have not been socialized to the
middle-class norms concerning happiness, mental illness, and prejudice. While lower-class respondents also desire the approval of
the interviewer, they may be less aware of the extent to which they
have different sets of norms. That this alternate explanation may be
correct is at least partially supported by the studies of Dohrenwend
(1966) and of Phillips and Clancy (1970) cited in Chapter II.

One of the problems with trying to understand the social
desirability effect in survey research is that very little is known as
to whether respondents react (a) to generalized (societal or sub-
cultural) norms, or (b) to what they see as the interviewer's beliefs.
In a recent exchange of views on this issue, Dohrenwend (1969),
J. Williams (1969) and Weiss (1969) have expressed their differences on this matter. Dohrenwend and Weiss share the opinion
that respondents usually react to generalized norms rather than
those of the interviewer. Thus, in their view, bias is always in the
direction of what the respondent sees as the normative (that is,
societal) expectations for someone like himself. J. Williams (1969:
125), on the other hand, states his anticipation that a respondent
will bias his answers "in the direction he believed would conform
to the opinions of the interviewer when (1) the respondent perceived
that a false response would result in 'reward' and/or (2) he perceived that a truthful answer would result in 'punishment'." Williams, therefore, sees the respondent as searching for cues from
the interviewer concerning *his* views of the best or most socially
desirable response.

It seems likely that both generalized norms and the respondent's perception of the interviewer's position exercise an influence on the respondent's replies. The important question, as J. Williams (1969: 125) notes, is "What might the respondent expect to gain or lose by falsifying a response?" There would seem to be a number of reasons for a respondent to falsify his responses. Principal among these, in my view, is the gaining of social approval from the interviewer. But there are other reasons, as well: to preserve his own self-image, to avoid feelings of personal discomfort or apprehension which frequently result from revealing one's thought or feeling to another (Summers and Hammonds, 1969), to resist the possibility of having the interviewer reveal to other people what he, the respondent, has said. These are, in fact, *the very same reasons for giving false reports in other everyday activities.* For as Goffman (1969:81) notes:

> There can hardly be a person who has never been concerned about giving his social or personal identities away, whether through lack of emotional and intellectual self-control, or the failure to inhibit expression, or the acknowledgement of a social relationship he was not supposed to have, or the demonstration of incongruous social practices.

What reasons are there, then, for a respondent to respond truthfully to an interviewer? For one thing, it is probably easier for most people to answer truthfully to some questions than to lie, in that telling a falsehood places the individual on his guard lest he respond inconsistently should he be asked the same question later on in the interview. Also an individual may respond honestly to an inquiry because the result of not doing so would be a loss of integrity and self-respect. And under certain circumstances the truth may be the safest response. If the respondent believes that he may be found out if he lies, he may regard the truth as the preferable response. Usually, of course, in the interview situation as in everyday conduct, an individual must weigh the possible costs and rewards ensuing from various responses and decide accordingly. To answer an interviewer's question truthfully may make a respondent feel proud but he may incur the interviewer's disapproval. To falsify a response may gain the respondent the interviewer's approval but the respondent may suffer a loss of integrity.

As do men in other social activities, respondents in social surveys may sometimes fabricate the answers which they give to the interviewers' questions. This being the case, we should consider the conditions under which a respondent's expectations of either positive or negative sanctions become so great that he finds it advantageous to falsify a response. I suspect (and I am aware of no empirical evidence on this matter) that a respondent is most apt to falsify his responses under one of two conditions: (1) when he strongly desires the social approbation and approval of the interviewer, or (2) when he has reason to fear the interviewer.

Taking first the situation where he wants the interviewers' approval, this will occur where there is some affective tie or bond between the respondent and the interviewer. When I speak here of "some affective tie or bond," I am speaking specifically of brief encounters such as those characterized by the interview situation. In more permanent and longer-established relationships—as between, say, husband and wife or between people who are good friends—individuals are much more able, and willing, to reveal certain misdeeds or feelings or to act in ways that may lead to the temporary loss of liking and social approval. That is, in *established* relationships there is a reservoir of feelings (both positive and negative) that makes considerations other than immediate social approval paramount in one or another interaction.

In the case of the survey interview, however, people may falsify their responses because the affective tie between respondent and interviewer is of only short duration. Such a relationship would seem to be most apt to occur when they share some meaningful status(es) or when there exists a high degree of rapport between them. There are numerous statuses on which they may be similar or dissimilar: age, sex, education, race, and social class, for example. They may also be similar on some statuses and dissimilar on others. For purposes of illustration here, however, I will consider only one status-attribute which they may or may not share: social class position. Where the interviewer and respondent share the same class status, I suggest that the respondent will be more likely to desire the interviewer's social approval than where their class statuses are dissimilar. With regard to the second condition mentioned above where a respondent is likely to falsify his response—when he fears the consequences of giving an honest response—that will probably be most likely to occur when the respondent occupies a lower class position than the investigator.

In addition to the similarity or dissimilarity of social class statuses for the interviewer and respondent, another important factor which plays a part in the interview situation is the extent of rapport between them. While the importance of good rapport is stressed in most methodology textbooks, there has also been some recognition of the possible biasing effects of "over rapport" (Dohrenwend et al., 1968; Hyman, 1954; C. Weiss, 1968; Williams, 1964, 1968). Hyman (1954:46–48) hypothesized that some interviewers tend to develop too much rapport with their respondents, because of ". . . a tendency to want to enter deeply into the respondents' affairs, which naturally increases the orientation of the respondent in the direction of the interviewers." These interviews, according to Hyman, tend to bias their respondents' answers. A more recent study by C. Weiss (1968) revealed that the better the rapport between investigator and respondent, the greater the proportion of biased responses. These studies suggest that too much rapport results in the interviewer and respondent treating one another as persons who are concerned with gaining approval and liking.

Let me speculate now as to how the two factors of social class status and rapport may together affect the respondents' falsification of answers. Although, as shown in previous chapters, a host of other factors are involved in the interviewer-respondent relationships, even a consideration of only these two factors is rather complex. In the discussion that follows, it is useful to speak not of the social class statuses of the interviewer and respondent but rather of the social status of the respondent *relative* to that of the interviewer. Although there are some few instances in which the respondent has a higher class standing than the interviewer does, it is much more frequently the case that one of two conditions prevails: (1) they occupy equal class statuses, or (2) the respondent has a lower class position than that of the interviewer. Hence, these two conditions together with the condition of either high or low rapport result in four combinations of relative status and rapport.

Figure 1 presents the four combinations of these two variables. Each of the four cells contains my estimate as to the amount of respondent falsification to be expected under each of the four conditions. Before discussing them, it should first be emphasized that the two independent variables, relative status and rapport, are apt to be rather strongly related to one another. That is, high rapport is likely to be associated with similar class statuses and low rapport with dissimilar statuses. The reason for this is that people's friendships are generally with persons of a similar socioeconomic status, in that people who share the same class position are likely to also possess the qualities that make them attractive to one another. However, in the interview situation it is possible that the interviewer, as part of his training and instructions, will sometimes strive for a high degree of rapport with the respondent—irrespective of their relative statuses. This being so, the relationship between rapport and the relative statuses of the two individuals will probably be less strong than in the majority of everyday activities.

Figure 1.   Respondent Bias: By Status of Respondent Relative to Interviewer and by Extent of Rapport

(Expressed in degree of bias)

| Extent of Rapport | Relative Status of Respondent | |
	Same	Lower
Low	Weak bias	Strong bias (threat of vulnerability)
High	Strong bias (desire for approval)	Strong bias (threat of vulnerability and desire for approval)

Turning now to Figure 1, let us consider first the upper left-hand cell. This depicts the situation where the interviewer and respondent share a similar class position, but where rapport between them is very weak. Although the lack of objective social distance between them might be expected to lead to a strong bias, the lack of rapport works in opposition to this expected tendency. The fact that they share the same class position means that the interviewer presents little threat to the respondent, while their lack of rapport means that the respondent is not apt to be very concerned with gaining the interviewer's approval. It seems unlikely, therefore, that the respondent will greatly falsify his answers to the interviewer's questions.

The second situation to be considered in Figure 1 is the upper right-hand cell, where the respondent has a low social class status relative to the interviewer and where there is a general lack of rapport between them. It would seem, as Williams (1968·125) has suggested, "that relatively great social distance (with the investigator having the higher status) would generally be associated with greater perceived threat and vulnerability on the part of the respondent." This may especially be the case when the relation is characterized by a lack of rapport—in that rapport would probably serve to reduce the respondent's fear of threat and vulnerability arising from his lower status. Here, then, there is apt to be a strong tendency for respondent bias due to fear rather than a desire for social approval.

The next point of interest is the lower left-hand cell, where the interviewer and respondent share the same class status and where there is a high degree of rapport between them. It is here that we find a strong possibility of respondent falsification due to a desire for social approval. For these present the maximal conditions under which the respondent is likely to be attracted to the interviewer. He may attempt to answer questions in such a way as to be consistent with what he perceives as the interviewer's preferences, in order to maintain or even increase the reward value of the interaction.

Finally, we turn to an examination of the fourth cell in Figure 1. the one which combines high rapport with a lower class status on the part of the respondent. Predictions about respondent bias are more difficult here than with the other three combinations. While we would expect a respondent to falsify his responses (a) because of threat and vulnerability when his status is lower, and (b) because of a desire for social approval when rapport is high, it is not clear how these tendencies operate when both factors are present. It may be that these two tendencies toward bias partially neutralize one another, thus resulting in a low degree of respondent falsification. Or it may be that they operate in a cumulative manner. If this is true, then the respondent is likely to falsify his answers so as to receive the social approval of the "threatening" interviewer. Of the two possibilities—toward neutralization and toward a cumulative effect—it would appear that the latter is the more likely possibility. Thus, a strong respondent bias is predicted in an interview situation characterized by high rapport and a lower class status on the part of the respondent.

Both the difference in the investigator's and respondent's class standing and the extent of rapport between them can be conceptualized in terms of differences in social distance between them. Although the line of thinking outlined above differs somewhat from that of Dohrenwend and her associates (Dohrenwend, 1969; Dohrenwend et al., 1968), the conclusions are consistent with their suggestion (Dohrenwend et al., 1968:419) that "in the interaction of interviewer and respondent there can be either too much social distance, or too little." This notion of the social distance between the investigator and respondent is a useful one, but it tends to minimize the importance of the source of social distance as it relates to respondent falsification on *certain kinds* of questions. It would appear, for instance, that respondent bias due to threat and apprehension (associated with interviewer-respondent status disparities) might be found most often with questions of a factual nature (e.g., whether one is registered to vote or contributes to the Community Chest), while bias due to the respondent's desire for social approval (associated with similar statuses and high rapport) may be found with questions pertaining to his attitudes, feelings, or mental states (Would you vote for a Negro? Are you bothered by nervousness?). Depending on the respondent's status relative to that of the interviewer, on the amount of rapport between them, and on the nature of the questions asked, sometimes the truth (as the respondent knows it) will be the best answer and sometimes a lie will be best. What this means, then, is that a respondent will falsify some questions and answer truthfully to others, even within the same interview situation. This should not be surprising in that it is exactly the way people act in most everyday social activities.

My discussion in the last few pages has centered on differences in the class status of investigator and respondent, on the amount of rapport between them, and on the types of questions asked—all as they may affect the amount of respondent falsification in the interview situation. There are, as we know, a host of other factors that play a part in determining the respondent's reports and answers. Among those discussed in Chapters II and III were: the race of the interviewer and respondent, their ages, sexual statuses, ethnicity, facial appearance, physical appearance and stature; the respondent's need for approval and tendencies toward yeasaying or naysaying; the interviewer's expectancies as regard the respondent's reports; and the physical settings in which investigations are conducted. It is clearly impossible to advance any overall formulation which would include the various effects of all of these factors, considered either alone or in combination. Were it possible to do so, sociologists would already possess the principles of social interaction which they are striving to discover.

To restate the main thesis of this chapter: as people do in many other social situations, respondents in survey studies make certain judgments about the interviewer based on a wide variety of signs given and given-off. These judgments concern who the interviewer is, what the respondent may expect of him, and what the interviewer expects or desires from the respondent. This being my view, let me conclude this chapter by briefly considering the interviewer-respondent relationship in somewhat more formal terms. In doing so, I draw on Goffman's (1969) most recent book where he has argued that face-to-face interaction can be better understood by examining the calculative game-like aspects of people's actions when they come together. He suggests that there are five basic moves in such mutual dealings or "expressions games," as Goffman calls them. I intend here to examine the relationship between interviewer and respondent in terms of such moves.

The first move is what Goffman calls an *unwitting move.* This occurs when people are, for all practical purposes, unaware or unconcerned about being observed; i.e., when an individual's observable behavior is unoriented to the assessment another individual might be making of it. As Goffman (1969:11) notes, "Such activity is at once part of the expression game and not part of the game and requires a paradoxical title." Thus, the potential respondent in answering the knock or ring of the survey interviewer may—in this initial contact—be generally indifferent as to how he appears in the eyes of the interviewer.

The second move in the interaction is termed a *naive move* by Goffman and, in the illustration here, is restricted to the interviewer. This refers to the assessment the interviewer makes of the respondent when he believes that the respondent can be taken as he appears; i.e., that the respondent is involved in an unwitting move. This move is probably found in the period prior to the start of the actual interview when the interviewer explains the purpose of the interview to the respondent.

Move three occurs when the respondent begins to engage in an intentional effort to produce expressions that he thinks will improve his situation in the eyes of the interviewer. These *control moves* are, of course, calculated and fully conscious efforts by the respondent. Wishing to appear healthy, well informed, unprejudiced, or whatever, he engages in impression management. He perceives his own activity from the interviewer's point of view, so as to exert control over it. Obviously there are differences among various respondents (as among other persons) in their awareness of what the interview is intended to measure or get at. Whatever their definitions of the situation, however, respondents are likely to concern themselves with controlling the cues, clues, and information provided to the interviewer.

In the fourth basic move, the interviewer performs what Goffman (1969:17–18) terms an *uncovering move:*

> The observer, suspecting that what he might have treated as an unwitting move is actually or possibly an obfuscation or misrepresentation, suspecting that what appears to be ingenuous fact could be shot through and through with a gamesman's manipulation and design, suspecting this, he can attempt to crack, pierce, penetrate, and otherwise get behind the apparent facts in order to uncover the real ones.

Thus, in an interview designed to get at people's past and present mental health status, for example, a respondent may answer "no" to questions asking whether he has ever been troubled by mental or nervous disorders. The interviewer, suspecting that the respondent may be misrepresenting his actual experiences, engages in an uncovering move by asking him to provide a list of all his contacts with medical personnel and facilities. Or he may query him about various troubles that he, the interviewer, has learned to see as symptoms of mental illness

The final move is what Goffman calls a *counter-uncovering move.* Just as respondents are aware that they must sometimes obfuscate or misrepresent what they perceive as the true facts, so they are also aware that they can be found out. Because of this possibility, they sometimes engage in counter-uncovering moves. Imagine, for instance, that the respondent who initially answers "no" to questions about mental and nervous disorders, later on in the interview answers affirmatively to questions about certain troubles that he has experienced. Imagine further that, having done so, he suddenly comes to realize that these are the kinds of questions that he once read—in college psychology or sociology courses, in *Reader's Digest,* or elsewhere—are intended to find out whether or not people have certain nervous or mental disorders. He might then attempt to react to the fact that he has been found out by asserting: "I know that those are the kinds of questions asked to find out if people are mentally ill. If that's why you are asking me about them, it won't tell you much—because when I answered 'yes' to several of them, what I had in mind was how I felt in certain stressful situations. You know, like when my mother died, when I was in combat, and during the time we thought my daughter might have cancer."

Although Goffman argues that this is the final move in expression games, and consequently in the interview as an example thereof, we can easily imagine interactions where the actors engage in counter-counter-uncovering moves or, even, counter-counter-counter-uncovering moves. In any case, Goffman's examination of the calculative nature of social interactions is useful in formalizing somewhat the social processes involved when interviewers and respondents come together in survey studies.

It should be clear from Goffman's analysis and from the earlier contents of this chapter that not all of the moves in an interaction are *real* ones. That is, there are what Goffman refers to as "virtual" or "tacit" moves. With the interview situation described above, the interviewer may imagine the likely consequence of the respondent discovering that his mental health status is being assessed and may attempt to counteract the respondent's attempt at misrepresentation before it occurs. Similarly, the respondent may attempt to counter moves that have, in fact, not been made. In short, interviewers and respondents alike—in common with all individuals—frequently act on the basis of a tacit interplay of moves.

What is most important for our interests here, however, is the fact that the respondent's moves (real or tacit) involve some concern with what is considered appropriate or inappropriate behavior for people occupying various statuses. Thus the respondent must always ask himself: What does someone like him (the interviewer) expect of someone like me in a situation like this? His answer to this broad inquiry will play a large part in determining how he reacts to the interviewer's questions, and to the consequent validity of survey results based on interviews.

Chapter V

The Use and Improvement of the Interview in Survey Research

The previous chapter focused on some of the social processes which may operate in the most prevalent of sociological data-collection procedures: namely, the survey research interview. From that discussion, and my discussions in earlier chapters, I conclude that surveys using interviews have several important limitations. Among them are the following: (1) they are subject to the influence of distortions and bad memories (what Riley, 1963, calls a "biased viewpoint effect") on the part of respondents; (2) they are affected by interviewer bias, also called "control effects"; (3) they can only obtain material that respondents are willing and able to report; (4) they obtain data from individuals; and (5) they fail to consider interaction.

These limitations, as I have stressed throughout, are of considerable significance. But the chief weakness of survey interviews is that they are *inappropriate* for the study of many, if not most, social phenomena of interest to social scientists. There are, however, instances where the survey interview *is* the most appropriate (and sometimes the only) procedure for gathering sociological data. Thus in the present chapter I would like to touch very briefly on some of the particular advantages of survey interviews, to mention some important studies that have utilized them, to speculate about their widespread utilization, and to make some suggestions for their improvement.

Surveys using interviews are assumed to have the following definite strengths: (1) they allow for gathering information concerning people's past behavior, such as voting practices and childhood experiences; (2) they are almost the only device by which the investigator can obtain data concerning certain private actions, such as sexual activities; (3) they allow for the study of motives, beliefs, values, and attitudes—things "inside" an individual that are often not directly reflected in observable behavior or appearance (Richardson et al., 1965); (4) they can be used with almost all segments of the population (Selltiz et al., 1959); (5) they provide for the collection of data from a large number of persons in a relatively standardized manner, thus ensuring quantification; (6) the data are amenable to statistical treatment (Galtung, 1967); and (7) they allow for generalizing to known populations.

Over the years, social scientists have conducted a number of important investigations based on the utilization of survey interviews. Among the best of these are studies of political behavior (Campbell et al., 1960), fertility and family planning (Freedman et al., 1959), consumer behavior and family income (Katona, 1960), religious attitudes and behavior (Lenski, 1963), and sexual behavior (Kinsey et al., 1948). Clearly, to secure data from large numbers of persons concerning such things as their private behavior (voting or sexual behavior), their attitudes and views (concerning religion and occupational prestige), or their future intentions (family planning), the survey interview appears to be a highly appropriate technique for collecting data.

Although survey interviews may be *appropriate* for such investigations, this does not mean that they are free of the limitations mentioned earlier. Let me consider as an example of interview weaknesses or limitations, simple descriptive surveys. These are designed not to discover causal relationships but rather aim to provide true quantitative descriptions of various aspects of a universe of people. Some of these descriptive surveys have as their goal obtaining such demographic data as population, age, marital status, income, and so forth. The best illustration of this type of survey is the U.S. Census. Cannell and Kahn (1968:527) remark on this as follows:

> Perhaps the prototypical example of research interviews is provided by the national census. Most countries of the world conduct some kind of population count, and in many countries the census has been expanded to provide with regularity an inventory of social resources and problems. *Census interviews usually make only modest demands on interviewer and respondent. They are brief; they ask for demographic data well within the respondent's knowledge and not of a kind which he is likely to regard as confidential.* Moreover, the information is requested under circumstances familiar to or expected by most respondents, and the request is backed by the legitimate power of the national government. (Italics added.)

According to Cannell and Kahn, then, census data secured through research interviews are obtained under almost idyllic conditions. This being the case, we would expect to find a high degree of accuracy in these data. Unfortunately, though. there has been very little evidence pertaining to the extent of accuracy in census reports.

There is available, however, a recent study which sheds considerable light on this matter. Hambright (1969) reports on an investigation where a sample of death certificates was matched with the 1960 census records, thus allowing for a comparison of response data for items asked on both records. The data on the two records were compared for the same persons. Inconsistencies between the two could have resulted from errors on either death or census records. although there was no way of determining where the errors lay. Hambright (1969:419) found a very low extent of disagreement with regard to color and nativity. There was disagreement for less than 1 per cent of the white respondents and only 2.3 per cent of the Negro respondents. And there was less than 2 per cent disagreement as to whether people were native- or foreign-born, although there was considerably more disagreement as to the exact country of origin. This could, of course, have come about through changing national boundaries and lack of knowledge as to where someone was born.

. However, there was considerable disagreement between death certificates and census records on the other two items of information investigated: age and marital status. When people's ages were compared for a specific age, there was disagreement among 27.3 per cent of the white males and 35.0 per cent of the females, and among 57.0 per cent of Negro males and 65.9 per cent of Negro females (Hambright, 1969:417). This is a high degree of disagreement, but is perhaps not surprising. After all, many people cannot easily recall whether their age is 34 or 35 or 36. Some individuals do not know their exact ages at all, and many people's exact ages are not known to their friends and relatives who may be responsible for providing information for death certificates. But even when people's ages were compared in terms of ten-year intervals (Hambright, 1969:417) there was considerable disagreement between death certificates and census records: 8.1 per cent for white males and 11.4 per cent for white females, and 23.8 per cent for Negro males and 30.3 per cent for Negro females.

As mentioned above, there was also quite a bit of disagreement with reports of marital status (Hambright, 1969:420). For instance, the two sets of records failed to coincide in terms of the single status of 9.0 per cent of white respondents and 21.6 per cent of Negro respondents. With the category of divorced, the records were in disagreement with the reports of 26.5 per cent of the whites and 42.4 per cent of the Negroes.

What Hambright's (1969) study shows, then, is an extremely small degree of disagreement on reports of color and nationality, and a considerable degree of disagreement on reports of age and marital status. The source of the disagreement is, as stated earlier, unknown. Nor is there any way of ascertaining the reasons for disagreement. But it seems obvious that people's reports concerning such data "well within the respondent's knowledge and not of a kind which he is likely to regard as confidential" (Cannell and

Kahn, 1968:527) *are subject to considerable inaccuracy.*[1] This being the case, we should not be surprised to find extreme inaccuracy in reports of other social phenomena.

Given that there is a good deal of inaccuracy, it is still the case that the survey interview is the most appropriate method for securing certain types of data. How else can we obtain information concerning such demographic data as age and marital status, such private acts as sexual activities and voting behavior, such mental contents as attitudes, beliefs, and opinions? Clearly, then, some attention must be given to ways of improving the validity of survey data.

Before considering the matter of the improvement of survey studies, however, I want to briefly review the central thesis of this book. Throughout this report, the argument has been made that most data-collection activities are instances of social interaction, and that the effects of such interaction must be taken into account by the sociologist. This means that a social scientist's methods are themselves usually unknown features of the findings which their use generates. It also has been stressed in the preceding pages that, in survey research, the processes involved in the interaction of interviewer and respondent are the same processes which are involved in other everyday activities. As in other social situations, individuals make an assessment as to the rewards, costs, and profits they may realize by acting in a given manner. Responding to various signs given and given-off, they make judgments about what they can expect of another person and what he expects of them. They consider the possible rewards (social approval, self-respect, etc.) that will ensue from various responses or behavior, as well as the possible costs (social disapproval, loss of self-respect, threats)

---

[1] An alternative explanation is that those (next-of-kin and friends) supplying information about the deceased simply do not know the details of marriage and age concerning people close to them. This probably accounts for some of the discrepancies in the two reports, although I would think these others would have been as familiar with the marital status of the deceased as with their nativity. But even the idea that those supplying the information do not know people's ages and details of marriage has implications for some sociological research, especially that concerned with proxy reports by certain individuals regarding details about the characteristics and behavior of other family members (as is the case, of course, in the U.S. Census).

resulting from different verbal and nonverbal behaviors. The respondent strives to perform in such a way as to maximize the profits to be earned in his exchange with the interviewer. Both the interviewer and the situation itself are, therefore, appraised in terms of the ratio of costs and rewards.

While some of the behavior which people exhibit in their interactions with others is unselfconscious and represents an almost automatic, though socially acquired, response to certain social and situational stimuli, much behavior represents a calculated and fully self-conscious desire to present oneself in the best possible manner. In the case of the survey interview situation, I have stressed in these pages my belief that the respondent is influenced both by generalized norms and by what he perceives as the interviewer's beliefs and expectations. Thus, much purposeful distortion occurs within the interview situation as the respondent attempts to adhere to one or another (sometimes contrary) set of social norms and expectations. This distortion or falsification of responses is especially likely to occur in instances where the interviewer is asking questions about certain so-called deviant behaviors, for example, mental illness, homosexuality, and criminal activity. In these instances, many people will fail to report or admit to behaviors or feelings that will define them as deviant—both in the eyes of the interviewer and in their own eyes as well.

Consider, as an instance, survey studies of the true prevalence of homosexual behavior. In American society when two adult males are seen kissing, holding hands, or engaged in sexual relations with one another, it is likely that they will be labeled homosexual (Kitsuse, 1964) and will probably be treated as such by others who have witnessed, or heard about, their behavior. They may also come to define themselves as homosexual, which they might not have done were it not for the public definition. Now imagine a young man being interviewed in a survey—typically by a young graduate student or a middle-class housewife. For purposes of argument, let us say that the young man *has* had sexual relations with another male but has never been witnessed or found out by others (i.e., he is not a deviant). The interviewer asks him if he has ever engaged in sexual relations with another male. Assuming that he is aware of the societal definition of homosexuality, he may very well answer "no." If he does answer no (that is, lies), he might feel ashamed for not having told the truth, and his sense of integrity may perhaps suffer. On the other hand, if he were to answer "yes," he might feel virtuous for having told the truth. But by answering affirmatively, he would also have placed himself in a position where he could be labeled homosexual and where he would risk the interviewer's disapproval, as well as perhaps placing himself in a threatening position (i.e., the interviewer might tell other people). Also, by admitting it to himself in the presence of another, he *defines himself* as homosexual.

The perspective of the above argument is, of course, consistent with explanations of deviance set forth by Becker (1963) and others (Erikson, 1962, Lemert, 1951, 1967, Scheff, 1966). In this view, deviance is to be seen not just as a quality of the acts a person commits, but rather as a consequence as well of the way that the public or certain designated experts respond to them. It would seem that when actors and witnesses are aware of the cultural standards of appropriateness that obtain in and for different status categories, we can expect to find that they will generally be inclined to avoid, and will be capable of not carrying out, such acts as would lead others to respond to them negatively. Thus, as has been emphasized, it may be that differences in the prevalence of some types of acts defined as deviance, among people who occupy different statuses, reflect differences in the actors' willingness to engage in or make visible certain actions or behaviors.

Let me now offer a somewhat more benign example than that of homosexuality, one involving voting behavior. My review of the literature on invalidity and bias in Chapter II indicated that many people claim to have voted when they actually have not. Once again, fabrication should not be unexpected. For there exists in American society—especially among the better educated—a strong normative expectation that people *should* get out and vote on election day. Assuming that the respondent in a voting survey is aware of the societal view concerning the desirability of voting, and assuming further that he is anxious to respond in a manner that he thinks will please the interviewer, he may falsely claim to have been among those who voted in the election in question. In such an instance, the respondent may lose a certain amount of self-respect, but he may feel that this is more than compensated for by his having assured himself of appearing as a good citizen in the eyes of the interviewer.

What these examples are meant to convey is that many of the measuring instruments used by sociologists are of questionable validity, either because the responses which they evoke correlate very weakly with some outside criteria or because the measures appear to correlate highly with some conceptually simpler variable (such as social class, intelligence, or social desirability).

THE WIDESPREAD USE OF INTERVIEWS

Before moving on to a discussion of some ways in which survey interviews might be improved, I am going to digress slightly in order to consider the question of why the survey interview has become the dominant research technique in sociology.

I am sure that most social scientists would agree that there is, in principle, no one data-collection procedure that is inherently right or best for collecting data about social phenomena. In fact, it seems to be a cardinal feature of methodology textbooks to present a list of basic criteria to be considered in choosing one or another research method. Richardson and his associates (1965), for example, suggest four criteria for weighing the relative merits of different methods: accessibility, economy of resources, accuracy, and relevance. I will discuss these criteria briefly before offering my own explanation for the widespread use of survey interviews.

Considering first the matter of *accessibility,* Richardson et al. (1965:22) observe that two separate questions are involved in the accessibility of information: "(1) Is the information obtainable at all by one of the . . . methods, regardless of the willingness of its 'proprietor' to make it available? (2) Will the 'proprietor' of the information be willing to make it available to the investigator?" The *economy of resources,* of course, refers to the cost of acquiring certain information. This cost represents an aggregate of the costs of four separate processes (Richardson et al., 1965:24): "(1) locating an appropriate source, (2) eliciting information from the source,

(3) editing, translation, digesting, and coding the information, and (4) carrying out the analysis so that the study provides answers to the questions originally posed by the investigator." With regard to *accuracy*, the investigator's task is to obtain the best (most reliable and valid) data possible at the least cost. That is, he must steer a course between high validity and reliability, on the one hand, and cost considerations, on the other. The final criterion mentioned by Richardson et al. (1965) concerns the *relevance* of any specific piece or set of data. Here, the investigator chooses a method of data collection on the basis of what will yield maximally relevant materials.

While I agree with Richardson and his associates that these four criteria for choosing a data-collection procedure *should* be considered by investigators, I do not think that the heavily disproportionate utilization of survey interviews in sociological research is to any great extent due to *serious* consideration of these criteria. Rather, it appears to me that the reasons for a heavy reliance on survey interviews lie elsewhere. These reasons will be set forth below, saving for the following chapters a lengthy discussion of the need to increase our utilization of alternate data-collection techniques.

First, sociologists have long been concerned that they be regarded as *scientists,* as is evident from a reading of the first chapter of almost any introductory textbook in sociology. This has resulted in a strong emphasis on the quantification of data, operational definitions, increasingly sophisticated techniques for the analysis of quantitative data and for the utilization of various statistical procedures. Nathan Glazer (1967:64) puts it as follows:

Unquestionably the great body of American sociologists see themselves as engaged in the building of a science. They believe that sociology should have operationally defined terms; it should have hypotheses and theories; it should have some predictive value; it should have practical application; its knowledge should accumulate; its theories, developed on the basis of tested bodies of empirical research in one historical setting, should be applicable in some measure to other settings; and it should develop the power and authority that physical and biological science have developed.

All of these are, it seems obvious, more easily accomplished with data obtained from large numbers of individuals through interviews than through observational studies. LaPiere (1969:42), who has long been critical of survey studies, suggests somewhat ruefully that they "have contributed immeasurably to the high status that sociology now enjoys, and that status is *prima facie* evidence of the wisdom of those who some thirty-odd years ago disregarded my doubts concerning the validity of these so-called 'objective' instruments of social measurements." This concern among many sociologists with fashioning themselves in what is, mistakenly (Kuhn, 1962), seen as the image of the physical scientist is undoubtedly one of the reasons for the widespread use of survey interviews.

A second reason is that it is, in most instances, far easier and less time-consuming for the investigator to collect data through interviews than it is to engage in the actual observation of behavior. If, for instance, we are concerned with social class differences in drug use, it is easier to have interviewers spend time obtaining reports through interviews with persons from different social class backgrounds than it is for the investigator to spend perhaps hundreds of hours of his own time—days and nights, weekdays and weekends—observing people from various social strata in order to witness, firsthand, those instances in which drugs are used. Related to this is the effort of many graduate students to gather data in a hurry, thereby allowing them to complete a thesis or dissertation in a minimal amount of time. And undoubtedly pressures toward publication often lead to the use of interviews as the preferred technique for obtaining data that will best result in quick publication.

Related to the above is the fact that many sociologists have access to large research centers with funds and personnel to engage in large-scale surveys. Such large-scale studies allow the investigator, as Jack Douglas (1970:219) notes: "to support many graduate students, who then do theses 'for him' on 'his project,' thereby multiplying and perpetuating the professional and social effect of this whole form of research."

Another important reason for the heavy use of interviews (and questionnaires as well) is that sociologists have generally failed to develop techniques for studying behavior *in situ.* This problem of how to study behavior taken together with the tremendous emphasis on survey techniques, has led to a general neglect of field methods courses in the curricula of most graduate departments of sociology. Hence, very few students have the opportunity for learning about observational methods. Not only are there few opportunities to acquire classroom instruction regarding the observation of behavior, but increasingly the student is required to spend a great deal of time mastering the use of quantitative techniques and learning to understand the application of such things as mathematical models. Blalock (1969b) and Borgatta (1969), among others, emphasize a need for more training in the "advanced technology" of sociology. This infatuation with punch cards, counter-sorters, and, more recently, magnetic tapes and computer programs, as well as statistical techniques and mathematical models, works against an interest in studying actual behavior. By concentrating on issues regarding the *analysis* of sociological data, attention is drawn away from the more crucial issues of *measurement.*

A final reason for the general stress on survey interviews, and the consequent neglect of observational studies, is the likelihood that a social researcher stands a better chance of having his research funded when he expresses, in his research proposal, an intention to interview a large number of persons than when he states an intention to observe behavior among a smaller number of individuals. A consequence of this, of course, is that few students get the opportunity to work on research projects with sociologists who are engaged in observational studies.

To my mind, the survey interview represents an almost perfect example of what Kaplan (1964:28) calls *the law of the instrument,* which he formulates as follows: "Give a small boy a hammer, and he will find that everything he encounters needs pounding. It comes as no particular surprise to discover that a scientist formulates problems in a way which requires for their solution just those techniques in which he himself is especially skilled."

Whatever the reasons for the great reliance upon the survey interview "hammer" among sociologists, it seems likely that this will continue to constitute the main, and often the sole, technique which sociologists will utilize in collecting data about the social phenomena which concern them. Thus it is important, at this point in the report, to consider some ways of improving survey data—especially with regard to their validity.

THE NEED FOR MORE VALIDATION STUDIES

An obvious need is for more studies concerning the validation of social science measuring instruments. Some idea of the paucity of such validation attempts can be seen from Straus's (1964:368) survey of family research instruments in which he found that, "all but a few of the 263 instruments surveyed were conceived without benefit of validating procedures." This would undoubtedly be the same case in most areas of sociological investigation, were they to be examined.

The first thing needed, if sociologists are to improve the validity of their measures, is an increase in the amount of what Summers and Hammonds (1969:120) call "primary validation data"—other observations of the respondents on the same variable(s), of which they (the respondents) have no knowledge and over which they have no control. Chapter II discussed some of these primary validation data: voting registration, records of election day turnout, clinic records, school records, files of the juvenile court. There are undoubtedly many more interview topics on which responses can be validated, including: income, educational accomplishments, marital status, church attendance, social participation, grade-point averages, reading habits, who a person's friends are, and attendance at various cultural activities. As Summers and Hammonds (1969:120) point out:

> Validation of this type is difficult and expensive at best; often it is impossible. Nevertheless, its rarity in respondent bias research constitutes a limitation to our understanding of such bias. We believe that a systematic and deliberate approach to the study of respondent bias could remove a good

deal of this limitation. This primary validation data would allow for a determination as to what kinds of (verifiable) topics people are most likely to be inaccurate about.

Of more importance, however, is a determination of the types of people who give the most inaccurate responses to various kinds of questions. It seems likely, for example, that adult women will falsify responses about their age more than will adult men. People with either very low or very high incomes may lie more about income questions than will persons at middle income levels. Primary validation data would also be useful for ascertaining what kinds of people respond falsely to what kinds of questions *under what circumstances.*[2] It is important to know, for instance, whether adult women give more accurate responses to questions about their age when asked by a female rather than a male interviewer, or an older interviewer rather than a younger one. Some other questions which demand answers are the following: Is the accuracy of respondents' answers concerning their marital status influenced by the divorce rate in the area where they live? Might not divorced persons more readily admit it if there is a high rate of divorce in their area (or if they perceive such a high rate) than if there is a low divorce rate? Are people's responses concerning mental hospitalization affected by public attitudes toward the mentally ill in their areas of residence? In that people's willingness to seek psychiatric assistance for emotional problems is affected by public attitudes toward the mentally ill (Jaco, 1960), it seems that their willingness to admit having sought such help in the past would also be influenced by their perceptions concerning public attitudes.

What is called for with the questions raised above is a kind of "contextual analysis" in which the dependent variable is the percentage of false responses (as determined by primary validation data) given by respondents, the independent variables are qualities of the respondents and interviewers, and the contextual variables are qualities of the environment.

To show how this might be accomplished, I offer a hypothetical

---

[2] Progress in this regard is being made by Cannell and his associates (Cannell and Fowler, 1963, 1964; Cannell et al., 1968).

example in Table I. In this table the dependent variable is the "percentage of divorced respondents giving false responses" on a question asking whether they have ever been divorced (as validated by official divorce records), the independent variables are the "sex of the respondents" and "sex of the interviewers," and the contextual variable is the "divorce rate" in the area in which the respondent lives. For purposes of illustration, I am assuming that: (1) people will give more accurate responses concerning divorce to an interviewer of the same than the opposite sex; (2) that men will admit divorce more readily than will women; and that (3) both men and women will be more likely to admit to being divorced where the divorce rate is high than where it is low. Thus, it can be seen in Table 1 that in an area with a low divorce rate, 50 per cent of the divorced women who are interviewed by men might falsify their responses. At the other extreme, in an area with a high rate of divorce, only 15 per cent of the divorced men who are interviewed by men may falsify their reports. While this kind of analysis involves the difficult task of collecting primary validation data, such analysis would tell us far more than we presently know about respondent bias.

Table 1.   Respondent Bias: By Divorce Rate, Sex of Respondent, and Sex of Interviewer

(% giving false responses)

	Divorce Rate			
	Low		High	
	Respondent's Sex			
Interviewer's Sex	Male	Female	Male	Female
Male	35%	50%	15%	30%
Female	45%	40%	25%	20%

INCLUDING THE INTERVIEWER
AS A FACTOR IN RESEARCH DESIGNS

While the validity of some sociological measuring instruments can be determined by obtaining primary validation data, other measures are not open to comparison with an outside criterion. But, as has been demonstrated throughout this report, they too are often of doubtful validity in that a wide range of factors other than those of explicit concern to the investigator may be influencing people's responses. Chief among these factors is the interviewer's influence on the respondent's replies. Galtung (1967:145) considers this problem when he notes that, "the simplest way of building a relevant factor into a design is by making it irrelevant." This, as he indicates, can be accomplished in three ways: (1) by *removing it,* (2) by *keeping it constant,* and (3) by *randomization.* The first technique, removing a relevant factor by, for example, using questionnaires in lieu of interviews, will not be discussed here since my focus is on the improvement of interview data.

The second technique can be accomplished in a number of ways: by extensive training that standardizes the interviewers, by selection of a very homogeneous group of interviewers, or by having one person do all the interviewing. Sociologists have generally emphasized this technique in dealing with interviewer influence, rather than that of randomization. In my view, there are some major weaknesses in trying to keep the interviewers constant. I do not believe that interviewers can be standardized in such a way that they operate as data-collecting machines, and, even if they could be, this results in the generation of data concerning people's responses to machines in survey research—not, in my opinion, a very interesting phenomenon. With regard to selecting homogeneous interviewers, we might consider these questions: What characteristics do we consider in regarding homogeneity? Do we try to select people who are of similar ages, social classes, sexual statuses, or what? And what combinations of these, and other attributes, do we consider with reference to homogeneity? Clearly, these are, at present, difficult questions to answer. However, I do see considerable merit in having all the interviewing done by the same person. A major problem here, of course, is that a single interviewer is simply not capable of securing a large number of interviews on his own.

It seems to me that the third technique for including the interviewer in the research design has considerably more merit than the one just discussed. Galtung (1967:145–146) remarks on this as follows:

The third method is the least costly and has the advantage that for large samples it also gives some opportunities for factorial *post hoc* analysis. Thus, one can examine attitude distributions for all combinations of the type age, sex, race of interviewer–age, sex, race of interviewee and all combinations of basic attitudes held by interviewers and by interviewees.

Friedman (1967:172–173) has suggested three ways of building the randomization of interviewers into the research design: (1) data collectors (in this case, interviewers) should be representatively sampled just as respondents are; (2) researchers should have samples of their data-collecting activities filmed; and (3) the contribution of the interviewer to the results can be assessed and corrected for by the regular use of *post hoc* methods of control. Friedman (1967:174) notes that, taken together, the three suggestions present this picture:

> The study is conducted with a representative sample of data-gatherers. A sample of the data-collecting sessions are filmed. The films are then analyzed to discover any activities which were in fact not controlled. When they are discovered, their contribution to the results can in fact be controlled by the use of either partial correlation or analysis of covariance, depending upon the nature of the research design.

Thus, *post hoc* and *a priori* methods of control are used together. Sociologists frequently, of course, use similar procedures in survey research; we randomly select our respondents, but also control for certain other variables in the analysis of our data. The merit of the suggestions of Galtung and Friedman is that they suggest that we do the same thing with our data collectors.

INCLUDING MEASURES OF
FREQUENTLY NEGLECTED VARIABLES

There is also the problem of determining the effects of several respondent variables usually excluded from sociological analyses:

for example, acquiescent response set and need for social approval. Measures of these variables can be obtained from the respondent in the course of the interview. Then, in the data analysis, the effects of these factors (both alone and in combination with attributes of the interviewer) on the relationships involving our principal independent and dependent variables can be assessed. Similarly, we can, and should, obtain (whenever appropriate) some measures as to the respondents' assessments of the desirability or undesirability of the phenomenon under study (for instance, mental illness, homosexual behavior, various kinds of crime, divorce, racial prejudice). The usefulness of such a procedure was shown in the study by Phillips and Clancy (1970) cited earlier, where it was found that respondents' assessments of the desirability of the items in a mental health inventory accounted for more of the variance in their mental health scores than did their social class standings. The chief problem in employing such additional measures is that they, too, are subject to bias and invalidity. Nevertheless, a heightened sensitivity to the existence of such a possibility can have only a salutary effect on sociological research.

CONSIDERING THE MEANING OF THE INTERVIEW

Another need is for further investigations as to the meaning of the interview situation for the respondent. An example of this regarding people's expectancies, or "evaluation apprehensions" as Rosenberg (1969) calls them, concerns the meaning of laboratory experiments for the subjects. An extension of this would be research to determine the meaning of various research situations and activities for different groups—social classes, ethnic groups, etc. The importance of such research was suggested 30 years ago by C. Wright Mills (1940a:320):

> Perhaps the central methodological problem in the social sciences springs from recognition that often there is a disparity between lingual and social-motor types of behavior. . . . [Systematic investigations] should enable the methodologist to build into his methods standard margins of error, different rates of discount for different *mileaux*. This

would show (for various cultural actions, types of subjects, and various modes of verbalization) how much and *in what direction* disparities between talk and action will probably go. In this way factual investigation should provide a basis for rules for the control and guidance of evidence and inference.

EXPERIMENTAL DESIGNS IN SURVEY SETTINGS

Stouffer (1950) and others have emphasized that the method of experiment presents the most powerful means yet devised to test a hypothesis and to establish causality. It would seem that sociologists might make heavy use of experimental designs in their research, in that there are serious questions about causal relationships based on survey data. As Hauser (1969:125) points out: "The 'causal' findings based on the analysis of interrelationships are suspect for at least two reasons: first, they often represent longitudinal inferences from cross-sectional data—always a dangerous procedure; and, second, they are based on procedures that only approximate, do not match, the logic of the experiment."

Under certain conditions, however, experimental and sample survey designs can be *combined* within a single study so as to obtain the advantages of both (Phillips and Wilson, 1967). In order to show how this might be accomplished, let us first consider some advantages and disadvantages of experiments and surveys. Kish (1959:328, 338) notes three important assets of experiments: (1) randomization controls the effects of confounding variables—an important consideration, as my earlier review of unwanted response determinants has clearly shown; (2) systematic introduction and variation of independent (in the sense that they are manipulable by the investigator) variables clarifies the direction of causation; and (3) use of these designs permits more flexible, efficient, and powerful statistical manipulation. At the same time, Kish argued, experiments have the following three important disadvantages: (1) it is often difficult to specify independent variables with sufficient precision so as to exclude all confounding extraneous variables; (2) samples used in experiments often do not systematically represent an important universe; and (3) measurements in experimental situations often cannot be made under the same conditions as in the natural settings of real populations.

Kish (1959:334) concludes from his comparison that, "In any specific situation one method may be better or more practical than the other; but there is no overall superiority in all situations for either method. Understanding the advantages and weaknesses of both methods should lead to better choices." While Kish's conclusion is obviously correct, it is important to emphasize that the use of one method does not necessarily preclude the use of the other. Sometimes it is appropriate and desirable to combine both methods, thereby gaining some advantages of each.

To illustrate the possibility of combining both methods, an example is taken from one of my earlier studies (Phillips, 1963). In discussing that study, technical statistical considerations are avoided since the main concern is with the utility of combining experimental and survey methods. Thorough treatments of these technical matters can be found in Finney (1960) and Lindquist (1953).

The study in question was concerned with determining the extent to which rejection of the mentally ill in urban society depends (a) on their disturbed behavior, and (b) on their having sought help for their difficulties. The problem of a design to make this determination will be discussed from three points of view: the naturalistic survey, the simple experiment, and the survey-experiment.

One way of approaching this problem would be to select a representative sample from the general population and to ascertain from each respondent whether he knew anyone who was mentally ill. Whenever a respondent said he knew such an individual, information would be obtained concerning the severity of the behavior disorder, the kind of help the ill person was seeking, and the degree to which the respondent rejected the designee. The difficulties with this approach are many and obvious. For example, it would be very difficult to find out whether a mentally ill person is known to the respondent without biasing later questions; there would be great difficulty in obtaining standardized measures of the severity of behavior disorders; in a random sample of the population some combinations of kind of help sought and degree of behavior disorder might occur too infrequently to permit analysis;

and, finally, the limitations of surveys noted by Kish are present—particularly the difficulty of removing confounding effects of extraneous variables. Consequently, although this natural survey approach is obvious, the difficulties with it are so apparent that it would probably not even be considered.

An entirely different way of approaching the problem is through a simple experimental design. For example, a convenient sample of subjects—say college sophomores—could be selected and divided randomly into subsets. Each subset could then be presented with a vignette depicting the behavior of a mentally ill person and the kind of help sought by him, and the degree of rejection could be measured by a social distance scale. The trouble is that this design does not meet the requirements of the problem, since the universe of college sophomores is not a very interesting one, and the research question posed concerns the rejection of the mentally ill in urban society generally. This design, then, would also not be satisfactory.

It is now evident that one solution to the difficulties might be to select a representative sample and conduct interviewing in usual survey fashion, but to build the content of the interviews around the presentation of vignettes. In this way, by using an experimental *technique,* we gain the representativeness of the survey while avoiding the problems inherent in relying on the experience of respondents with the mentally ill. And, in fact, previous research on rejection of the mentally ill has used this very technique (Cumming and Cumming, 1957; Dohrenwend et al., 1962; Lemkau and Crocetti, 1962; Star, 1957). However, the point to emphasize here is that *borrowing an experimental technique does not automatically result in an experimental design.*

For example, previous studies have used the vignette technique, but generally all respondents were given the vignettes in the same order. Certainly it is customary in survey research to ask every respondent the same set of questions in the same sequence, and often there are very good reasons for doing so. Indeed, this is one of the advantages of systematic surveys over more informal interviewing procedures. However, considered from the point of view of experimental design, presenting every respondent with the same vignettes in the same sequence may well amount to presenting every subject with the same stimuli. In other words, this procedure appears to be no experiment at all, since the essential characteristic of an experimental design is random allocation of subjects to *different* categories of the independent variables; i.e., to subsets presented with different stimuli.

The difficulties here can be seen more clearly if we consider the kinds of analysis that are possible. First, suppose there is only one vignette, which is presented to every respondent. In this case, one can study how rejection varies in different subsamples—e.g., among men and women, highly educated and less educated, etc. But of course no information is gained about how types of behavior or kinds of help-source affect rejection. Next, suppose there are, say, five types of behavior A, B, C, D, and E (for example, a paranoid schizophrenic, an anxious-depressed person), and five help-sources, 1, 2, 3, 4, and 5 (for instance, a physician, a psychiatrist). These can be combined in all combinations to yield twenty-five different vignettes. Again the variation of rejection (as measured by a social distance scale) between subsamples can be investigated, but if every respondent sees all twenty-five vignettes in the same sequence, it will be difficult to assess the effects of type of behavior and kind of help-source since there is no way of taking into account possible effects of respondents seeing the vignettes in a particular sequence. Thus, behavior A may be rejected most often because it happened to be seen first of all in combination with help-source 5, with the result that subsequent responses to behavior A combined with help-sources 1, 2, 3, and 4 are biased; or responses to behavior B may be biased because B is presented after A. In addition, there would be the important problem of fatigue were people to be faced with twenty-five different combinations of behavior and help-source.

It is evident, then, that the habits developed in ordinary survey research must give way to a more sophisticated approach when dealing with problems of this kind. We must, in fact, treat the problem as one in experimental design, even though the data are obtained from a survey. In the present instance, with twenty-five combinations of behavior and sources of help, one possible design is to divide the sample randomly into twenty-five subsamples and present each with only one combination of behavior and help-source. In this manner, order effects are eliminated, since each respondent sees only one vignette, and individual factors are controlled through randomization. A problem with this procedure, however, is that a very large sample is required; if, say, sixty cases are wanted in each combination, then a sample of fifteen hundred individuals (sixty times twenty-five) is necessary. Fortunately, this is not the only possible design; in fact, it was possible to find one that was very much more efficient.

The design which was ultimately employed is known as a "Graeco-Latin square" design. Although the statistical theory is complicated (Finney, 1960; Lindquist, 1953), the mechanics are quite simple, and it will be instructive to review the procedure as a specific illustration of the use of an experimental design in a survey context. With the form of the Graeco-Latin square design employed here, it is possible to evaluate the main effects of both independent variables and their joint effects without having to present more than five of the twenty-five combinations of behavior and help-source to any one respondent. This means that if sixty cases are wanted in each combination of the two variables, they can be obtained with a sample of three hundred respondents— rather than the fifteen hundred which would be needed if the preceding procedure were used. In addition to allowing determinations of magnitude of the relative and interactive effects of different categories of the two independent variables (behavior and help-source), the design counterbalances the effects of the order in which the combinations are viewed by the respondents and it randomizes the effects of extraneous variables. Moreover, the design fully utilizes the respondents, in that each contributes a score to the dependent variable for each of the five rows and columns.

In order to use this experimental design, a probability sample of three hundred respondents was randomly divided into five subsamples of sixty persons each. Each individual in each subsample saw five combinations of behavior and help-source, but no subsample or individual saw any given behavior or any given help-source more than once. Thus, using the Graeco-Latin square design, it was possible to classify the data into five categories on each of the two independent variables. In Figure 2, the numbers correspond to the various sources of help, and the letters to the

Figure 2.   The Graeco-Latin Square Design

Order				
Group 1 A1	B2	C3	D4	E5
Group 2 B3	C4	D5	E1	A2
Group 3 C5	D1	E2	A3	B4
Group 4 D2	E3	A4	B5	C1
Group 5 E4	A5	B1	C2	D3

different behaviors; the combinations of the two variables presented to each subsample and the orders of presentation are readily apparent.

There are many survey situations in which experimental designs may be appropriate and desirable. Although most survey research is concerned with the effects of some characteristics of the respondent on a dependent variable, there are other occasions where the investigator is concerned with characteristics or attributes of persons who are being judged or evaluated by the respondent. But even in these situations where the inclusion of experimental designs might be appropriate, they are usually not considered as applicable to survey research. A rather obvious reason for this is that, to most sociologists, experimental designs are restricted to situations where subjects are both readily available to the experimenter and are motivated to cooperate.

It is possible to list a wide variety of survey research topics for which experimental designs might be appropriate. For instance, if a researcher were interested in the extent to which (a) occupation and (b) race or ethnicity influence the subjective placement of individuals in the status hierarchy of American society, it might be desirable to combine various categories of these two variables (which are, of course, attributes of the person being evaluated) in an experimental design using case descriptions, as was done in the study of mental illness discussed above. Or an investigator interested in the degree to which a hypothetical candidate's (a) party affiliation and (b) religious affiliation influence people's intended vote, could easily combine these two variables in an experimental design.

However, the most intriguing use of the survey-experiment

might be in research designed to learn more about the data-collection process itself. For instance, subsamples of a larger sample could be randomly assigned to various experimental conditions— as represented by various combinations of *interviewer* qualities or characteristics. If one were interested in how interviewers' (a) friendliness and (b) knowledge of the investigator's hypothesis affected people's responses on various items, these two variables could be combined in an experimental design. For each of the two variables there might be three experimental conditions. Thus, for friendliness: friendly, neutral, and unfriendly; and for knowledge of hypothesis: correct knowledge, no knowledge and incorrect knowledge. This 3 × 3 design would tell us how these two variables, in various combinations, affect respondents' answers to various questions. The same procedure could, of course, be followed with other interviewer attributes: sex, age, social class position, ethnicity, etc. There are undoubtedly certain limitations in the use of experimental designs in survey research. Nevertheless, the employment of such designs by sociologists could take us a long way toward understanding various sources of bias in data-collection activities, and could help us greatly in increasing the validity of our measuring instruments.

IMPROVED TRAINING OF INTERVIEWERS

There is one additional step that must be taken if sociologists are to obtain more valid data from survey studies. That is the need for improving the training of those responsible for the actual interviewing of people in survey studies. Although in many instances interviewers are trained at some length so as to, hopefully, eliminate bias and invalidity, in other instances the training is minimal. For example, the New York Times (1969) reports the following with regard to census-takers for the year 1970. The 160,000 census-takers receive two days of classroom preparation from instructors who are required to read a 300-page manual to each of them. According to the Times' report, "Census-takers will be paid $2 an hour. Many of them will be recommended for the job by the Republican party organization, but others will be just plain applicants— the bulk of them housewives—who want a part-time job. The supervisory and executive positions in every census are filled 'with the advice of the party in the White House'." It seems obvious that these requirements and training procedures fall far short of what is necessary in terms of trying to obtain the best possible data about a great variety of questions.

Undoubtedly, there are other ways of improving the interview as it is used in survey studies. And it is certainly time that those proponents of the survey interview start to give more careful attention to this issue. Hopefully, the above discussion begins to suggest some possibilities for such improvement.

Chapter VI

Alternate Methods of Data Collection

In the previous chapter, the emphasis was on ways of improving survey studies based on interviews. As has been stated throughout this book, interviews along with questionnaires are the most prevalent types of data-collection techniques employed by sociological researchers. To repeat a central theme of this book: this means that much of our sociological knowledge ultimately rests upon people's reports of their behavior.

There are, however, data-collection procedures which attempt to avoid this heavy dependence on verbal reports, and I will discuss two of them in this chapter. One of these is a procedure frequently utilized by anthropological investigators; the other, a procedure that appears to be more often employed by psychologists than by sociologists. I refer here to participant observation techniques and unobtrusive measures. Like survey interviews, these two procedures are characterized by definite strengths and weaknesses. In my view, however, both of them have much to recommend them for the study of social phenomena. The remainder of this chapter will concern a discussion of these two techniques, while the final chapter of the book will examine in greater detail issues of personal involvement in the collection of data necessary to answer the kinds of questions that I believe should concern sociologists.

UNOBTRUSIVE MEASURES

Unobtrusive measures of social phenomena are methods of observation which directly remove the observer from the behavior, interactions, or events being studied. Such techniques as hidden observation (involving not only hidden investigators but also hidden recording devices and photographic equipment as well), contrived observations, trace analysis, and the examination of secondary records have been discussed by Webb et al. (1966) as ways of avoiding the contamination arising when investigators and research subjects confront one another in social science investigations. At least some of these techniques have the added advantage of allowing for the measurement of actual behavior and interaction, rather than relying upon people's verbal reports of their activities.

Webb and his associates (1966:175) point out that with these measures "the individual is not aware of being tested, and there is little danger that the act of measurement will itself serve as a force for change in behavior or elicit role-playing that confounds that data." An example of an unobtrusive measure, and one that is not discussed by Webb et al., is Milgram's (1969; and Milgram et al., 1965) "lost-letter technique." Milgram (1969:30–31) describes it as follows:

An investigator distributes—drops—throughout a city a large number of letters, addressed and stamped, but unposted. A person who comes across one of these "lost" letters on the street must decide what to do: mail it? disregard it? destroy it? There is a widespread feeling among people that one *ought* to mail such a letter. . . . In some circumstances, however—as when the letter is addressed to an organization the finder thinks highly objectionable— he may not mail it. Thus, by varying the addresses on the letters and calculating the proportion returned for each address, one can measure sentiment toward an organization.

The advantage of this technique, according to Milgram, is that it avoids many of the problems (some of which I have considered earlier) inherent in the survey interview, which is the usual method of assessing people's attitudes and sentiments. For in the lost-letter technique the respondent does not encounter an interviewer's questioning, but rather is presented with an opportunity to act in regard to an object with political and social attributes. A basic premise in Milgram's technique is that people's actions with regard to the lost letters will tell us something about how they relate to that object. By mailing the lost letter, say to the National Association for the Advancement of Colored People, he aids the organization in question. By disregarding or destroying a letter to the same or a different organization (for instance, the Communist Party), the individual hinders the organization. As Milgram emphasizes, what the individual does with regard to a lost letter defines his relationship toward an organization by the quality of his actions.

Another illustration of an unobtrusive measure is provided by Berkowitz (cited in Milgram, 1970) who was concerned with the tempo and pace of city life. In an attempt to get some idea as to whether various cities have an easygoing and leisurely quality or one frenetic and hectic, he conducted a series of investigations of walking speeds in a number of American cities as well as in smaller and moderate-sized towns. Thus, by measuring people's speeds in walking he was able to obtain an unobtrusive measure of the tempo of life in different cities and towns.

It seems obvious that there are many other circumstances where simple observations could be readily utilized. Denzin (1970:269–284) mentions five types of simple observations open to the investigator: (1) observations of exterior body and physical signs (e.g., clothing and hair styles), (2) the analysis of expressive movements (e.g., studies of eye and facial movements), (3) physical location analysis (e.g., the studies by Hall and Sommer described in Chapter III of this report), (4) observations of language behavior (e.g., tape-recordings of conversations), and (5) time-sampling analysis (e.g., observations of how people spend their time—perhaps based on samples of certain time segments). Some of these observational techniques can be utilized for the study of individual behavior, as when investigations are made of walking speeds in various locales or of pedestrian behavior at traffic lights. Some are useful for studying people in interaction with one another. Sommer's studies of seating patterns and Hall's investigations of distancing during conversations are examples of the usefulness of such observational techniques.

The above examples of unobtrusive measures avoid some of the pitfalls of typical survey research studies. In terms of Goffman's "basic moves" considered in Chapter IV, only two moves are involved in unobtrusive observations: "unwitting moves" by those being observed and "naive moves" by the investigator. But what are the general qualities that make a good nonreactive or unobtrusive measure? Sechrest (1968:574–575) lists three such qualities. First, it should bear a fairly evident relation to the variable that it presumably reflects. That is, very few inferential steps should be required to interpret the measure as an index of the variable of interest. Second, a good nonreactive measure must have the possibility of being observed in a nonlaboratory setting, and without suggesting the nature of the measurement to the subject(s) of research interest. And, third, the measurement process should not affect the variable, or underlying predisposition, being assessed. The main strength of these methods, when the above criteria are met, is that the individual is not aware of being studied and is unlikely, therefore, to change his responses or behavior in line with cues provided (both given and given-off) by the investigator. Thus the potential biases and invalidity created by the coming together of investigator and subject are avoided.

However, these methodological practices have two major weaknesses. The first concerns their external validity. It is difficult to estimate what can be generalized to other populations, situations, and measures on the findings. The second weakness is, in my view, more important. By focusing on overt physical behavior, as these unobtrusive measures frequently do, the social scientist utilizing an unobtrusive measure takes an extreme behavioristic stance. In removing himself from the flow of interaction, his inferences concerning the interpretations and definitions of the behavior are one step further removed from those social phenomena that concern him. Denzin (1970:261), too, has recognized this and suggests that: "the chief utility of unobtrusive measures is realized when they are combined with methods that probe the subjective factors of interaction."

But it seems clear that if these unobtrusive or nonreactive measures were used together with some of the precautions suggested earlier for survey studies, confidence in the validity of our results would be greatly increased. Webb et al. (1966) emphasize that no research method is totally without bias, and they suggest that interviews and questionnaires need to be supplemented by other methods which study the same variables of empirical concern. While recognizing that all social science measuring devices are subject to bias and invalidity, they argue (Webb et al., 1966:174) that when a hypothesis, for instance, "can survive the confrontation of a series of complementary methods of testing, it contains a degree of validity unattainable by one tested within the more constricted framework of a single method."

PARTICIPANT OBSERVATION TECHNIQUES

As I noted in the above discussion, unobtrusive measures are in many instances far preferable to survey interviews: they are frequently based on actual observations of behavior and interaction —observations made in such a manner as to avoid affecting the measures being obtained. However, they share with survey interviews and questionnaires the very important weakness of removing the investigator from those social phenomena which he is investigating. This means that when an investigator interprets the behavior in question, he often does so from a position of ignorance about the life and activities of those he is studying. Consequently, the correctness of his interpretations is often highly problematic. That is, the investigator always makes *some* interpretation of other people's conduct, but there is no assurance that his interpretation is correct.

As an example of this, consider studies of walking speeds. Imagine that we find that people in New York City walk faster than do people in Paris. Because we, presumably, know something about the two cities (having lived in, read about, or visited them), we would probably interpret our findings to mean that New York City has a generally more hectic nature while Paris has a more leisurely quality. We would interpret the differences in walking speeds as indicative of—and, perhaps, brought about by—more widespread differences in the tempo of life in the two cities. Clearly, however, such an interpretation is dependent upon our having some *prior knowledge* of city life in New York and Paris.

It would seem, then, that our interpretation of any empirical finding is dependent upon what we already know about the subject of investigation (or similar subjects). Thus if we were to have obtained data on walking speeds in two cities that we know nothing about—say, Athens and Peking—our interpretation of the data would be less likely to be correct than where we are already somewhat familiar with the phenomena under study. This familiarity with the persons, groups, institutions, or cultures of interest is obtained through the investigator's own, direct or vicarious, experience, and through acquaintance with history, literature, biography, and ethnography (Redfield, 1948). However, the most direct way of acquiring such familiarity is to *participate* in the symbolic world of those being studied. This recognition that researchers need to participate in order to get at the common-sense meanings shared by the members of any group or society gave rise to the participant observer methods developed by anthropologists and by sociologists of the "Chicago school."

Most social scientists who stress the importance of various forms of participant observation are concerned with what are seen as subjective aspects of social interaction. It is important here to spell out what I mean in my usage of this term. *Subjective* is, of course, the antonym of *objective* which is usually taken to mean true to the facts. I use the term *subjective* here, however, in the sense indicated by Nathanson (1970:56), "to mean related to a person, a 'subject' in the sense of an individual." It seems clear that the use of interviews and questionnaires reflects what is considered an objective attitude on the part of many sociologists interested in studying human behavior. This attitude—based on an acceptance of behaviorism, empiricism, and positivism—stresses the importance of hard data and exact measurement of social phenomena. Those holding this view assume that the world can be objectively known, that there are facts to be discovered out there in the real world. While this attitude seems to be the dominant one among sociologists, there are others who prefer an alternative approach to the study of social phenomena. They choose to approach the study of social phenomena from a subjective point of view.

In discussing these so-called objective and subjective approaches to the practice of sociology, it is important to precede my eventual discussion of observational methods by considering first the matter of "interaction" and "meaning." As was noted in Chapter I, the professed concern of sociology is with the study of social interaction. I take this to mean that sociologists are concerned with *inter*action, with *action* being seen as behavior that is meaningful to the actor (Parsons, 1937, 1951; Weber, 1947). Our interest is in interaction where two or more actors respond to one another's actions. Even sociologists who are concerned mainly with phenomena on the microlevel can be viewed as focusing on patterned interrelations among individual actors. Wilson (1970:698) puts it this way: "the process of interaction, then, is at the logical core of sociological interest, even though for some purposes, particularly of a macrosociological sort, this is often left implicit." And Weber (Gerth and Mills, 1960:55) asserts that "in general, for sociology, such concepts as 'state,' 'association,' 'feudalism,' and the like, designate categories of human interaction."

Although many sociologists are concerned with social interaction, they fail to get at it with their most frequently employed research techniques: questionnaires and interviews.[1] They typically obtain reports of behavior and interaction from one individual, then from another, and another, and so on, until each of the persons in their sample has been interviewed or has filled out a questionnaire. Individuals are then grouped together on the basis of some variables of theoretical interest to the investigator, and are discussed as if interaction had actually been studied. In addition to these limitations of interviews, especially in survey research, we have seen that the chief independent variables of interest to investigators in such studies explain only a small portion of the variance in their dependent variables. One reason for this, I have argued, is that the

---

[1] Whyte (1969a:47) notes that "we need data on social processes, and questionnaires do not provide such data. Who is to provide such data? Somebody who is out in the field observing what is going on, perhaps even a participant observer."

interview process itself constitutes a major (although how major is presently unknown) source of influence on the respondents' replies and reports.

There is, however, still a further limitation of questionnaire and survey interview techniques which has not yet been adequately discussed in the present report: the failure of sociologists to get at "meaning." This limitation is also found to varying extents in most other data-collection techniques common to sociology, but its relevance is most apparent for studies based on questionnaires and interviews in that these constitute the dominant modes of data collection in our discipline.

Before discussing this limitation, it is useful to locate it within the present dominant paradigm (Kuhn 1962) or world-view underlying sociology as it is practiced today. Kuhn argues that in every discipline there is a shared paradigm which commits its practitioners to the same rules and standards for scientific practice; in a sense, such paradigms provide a discipline's practitioners with a kind of map. However, paradigms do more than this, for as Kuhn (1962:108) notes: "paradigms provide scientists not only with a map but also with some of the directions essential for map-making. In learning a paradigm the scientist acquires theory, methods, and standards together, usually in an inextricable mixture."

One of the elements of this paradigm in sociology is the conception of social interaction which is held by its practitioners. The dominant view seems to be one in which people's acquired dispositions (attitudes, sentiments, personalities, etc.) are seen as working together with the role-expectations of their respective positions to explain interaction. The actor, from this viewpoint, is seen as an occupant of a position for which there is a specified set of rules (norms). Blumer (1966:542–543), whose view is similar to that of George Herbert Mead, describes this "structural conception"—which he, of course, opposes—as follows:

The conception presumes that a human society is structured with regard to (a) the social positions occupied by the people in it and with regard to (b) the patterns of behavior in which they engage. It is presumed further that this interlinked structure of social positions and behavior patterns is the overall determinant of social action; this is evidenced, of course, in the practice of explaining conduct by such structural concepts as role requirements, status demands, strata differences, cultural prescriptions, values and norms.

Central to the structural conception of interaction is the notion of *shared* symbols and meanings, including language and gestures, for this is what serves as a commonly understood median of communication for their interaction (Wilson, 1970). That is, there is an implicit assumption of a culturally established cognitive consensus (for instance, Parsons [1937, 1951] speaks of a "shared cognitive culture") that can be taken for granted by the investigator. An important consequence of this assumption is that the sociological researcher typically assumes that he knows the meanings of his measures (questions, indices, whatever) for those he is investigating, and that he understands what he is observing.

This dominant conception of interaction is very much different from the conception of interaction as an interpretive process (Blumer, 1954, 1956, 1966; Garfinkel, 1967; Turner, 1962). Those of the latter persuasion see interaction as an interpretive process in which meanings evolve and change over the course of interaction. For instance, Turner (1962:22) states that "since the role [by which he means a coherent pattern of behaviors] of alter can only be inferred rather than directly known by ego, testing inferences about the role of alter is a continuing element in interaction." And Blumer (1966:538) notes that "in the flow of group life there are innumerable points at which the participants are *re*defining each other's acts." This means, as Wilson (1970:700) points out, that "the perceived purpose and meaning in the other's actions are always provisional and subject to revision in the light of subsequent events in the course of interaction."

An important methodological consequence of an interpretive conception of interaction is clearly stated by Blumer (1966:542):

On the methodological or research side the study of action would have to be made from the position of the actor. Since action is forged by the actor out of what he perceives, interprets, and judges, one would have to see the operating situation as the actor sees it, perceive objects as the actor perceives them, ascertain their meaning in terms of the meaning they have for the actor, and follow the actor's line of conduct as the actor organizes it—in short, one would have to take the role of the actor and see his world from his standpoint.

Many sociologists sharing Blumer's view have been strongly influenced by the phenomenological movement. The distinctive feature of a phenomenological approach is its view that knowledge is sought through immediate, intuitive apprehension of human experience. Laing (1967:17) states that, "the task of social phenomenology is to relate my experience of the other's behavior to the other's experience of my behavior. Its study is the relation between experience and experience: its true field is *inter-experience.*" For phenomenologists like Schutz (1953, 1954) and Nathanson (1963) social reality is made up of the meanings which actors give to their actions and to their situations. The phenomenologists' position is that society is ordered by the social actors, not by the sociologist. Social actors produce social order in terms of *their* constructs. This means that to understand this order one has to attend to the social construction of *meanings.* Thus, the phenomenological approach includes a variety of positions which emphasize the primacy of consciousness and subjective meaning in the interpretation of social action. This view was clearly articulated by Max Weber (1947: 88) when he defined sociology as a science which

attempts the interpretive understanding of social action in order thereby to arrive at a causal explanation of its course and events. In "action" is included all human behavior when and in so far as the acting individual attaches a subjective meaning to it. Action in this sense may be either overt or purely inward or subjective: it may consist of positive intervention or acquiescing in the situation. Action is social in so far as, by virtue of the subjective meaning attached to it by the acting individual (or individuals), it takes account of the behavior of others and is thereby oriented in its course.

Central to Weber's view of sociology was an emphasis on *verstehen* which has as its goal finding out what the actor means in his action. Weber was, of course, interested in generalizations about various social phenomena. But his genius lay in his realization that *explanation*—in the sense of the correlation of external facts—was not sufficient for the social scientist. Rather, the social scientist should strive *to understand* the significance and meanings of those patterns and regularities for the persons involved. So, for instance, in *The Protestant Ethic and the Spirit of Capitalism* (1958), Weber concerned himself not only with demonstrating an association between religious affiliation and the accumulation of capital but also with grasping the religious motives ensuing from the ethical injunctions of ascetic Protestanism. To Weber, then, human behavior could not be comprehended without reference to the motivation of actors and to the meanings *they* impute to their action.

While this brief discussion is clearly inadequate for any deep understanding of phenomenology, it does provide for a comparison of the two dominant approaches to studying social phenomena. On the one hand, there are those (the majority of sociologists) who believe that the methods of the natural sciences are the only scientific ones, and that these methods must be applied to the study of social behavior. On the other hand, there are those who hold that there is a basic difference in the structure of the world of nature and the social world. Hence, from this viewpoint, the methods of the natural scientists—strictly applied—are inapplicable.

The influence of subjective and phenomenological approaches is most clearly seen in the methodology of observational studies, in which I include ethnomethodology. Although this influence is more explicitly apparent in ethnomethodology than in more traditional observational studies, the latter will be discussed first.

Various writers have defined participant observation in different ways, but the definition of Schwartz and Schwartz (1955:343) includes the essential elements common to all definitions.

For our purposes we define participant observation as a process in which the observer's presence in a social situation is maintained for the purpose of scientific investigation.

The observer is in a face-to-face relationship with the observed. and, by participating with them in their natural life setting, he gathers data. Thus, the observer is part of the context being observed, and he both modifies and is influenced by this context. The role of participant-observer may be either formal or informal, concealed or revealed; the observer may spend a good deal or very little time in the research situation; the participant-observer may be an integral part of the social situation or largely peripheral to it.

There is, of course, no one observational role employed by sociological field workers who seek out man in his natural habitat. However, Gold (1958) has listed four different roles for sociologists conducting field work: (1) the *complete participant,* where the true identity and purpose of the researcher are not known to those whom he observes, rather, as much as possible, he interacts with them in a natural manner in all areas of their life in which he has both an interest and access; (2) the *participant-as-observer* role, where both the field worker and informants are aware that theirs is a field relationship; (3) the *observer-as-participant* role, which, according to Gold, is used in studies involving one-visit interviews requiring relatively more formal observation than either informal observation or participation of any kind; and (4) the role of *complete observer,* where the field worker has no social interaction with informants, and tries to observe people in such a way that they are unaware of his observing them. These, then, constitute four roles for the field worker. As will be seen later in the following chapter, however, there are other ways of viewing the possible role of the field worker.

Some field workers have argued that in order to minimize the researcher's influence upon the social phenomena which he is engaged in describing, he must transform himself into a spectator who observes people's behavior but refrains from letting his own expectations, desires, interests, or purposes interfere with the behavior observed. Other investigators have recognized that even the best ethnographers and field workers cannot keep their expectations, interests, etc., silent. For example, Schwartz and Schwartz (1955:350–351) state that the issue is not whether he will become emotionally involved, but rather the nature of the involvement. The involvement, whether it is closer to one end of the continuum (sympathetic identification) or to the other end (projective distortion), is very little a function of the observer's role. Rather, it is primarily a function of his experience, awareness, and personality constellation and the way these are integrated with a particular social situation.

Field workers also differ with respect to their emphasis on the codification of procedures. Some field workers have attempted to provide such codification (Whyte, 1955), sometimes in rules (Becker, 1958), while others have argued that the very attempt to codify denies the inductive nature of such research operations (Glaser and Strauss, 1967).

One thing seems clear in distinguishing observational studies from survey studies based on interviews: observational studies make it possible to study behavior as it *occurs* rather than as it is *reported*. While survey interviews often assure standardization of verbal reports, observational techniques provide a more intimate view of social behavior and interaction. What this means, on the one hand, is that the field investigator, through his closer involvement with those he is describing, may be more apt than is the interviewer to influence those aspects of behavior that he wishes to study. On the other hand, however, the field worker is much better able than the interviewer to engage in a wide variety of what might be considered "validation procedures." That is, not only does he have a large number of signs given and given-off to consider, but he also can check an individual's behavior in a number of different contexts or situations in order to ascertain the stability of various behavior patterns, and also to assess the validity of people's verbal reports. This means that in his *direct* dealings and encounters with those he is studying, the game-like aspects of interaction described by Goffman (1969) will prevail. The investigator and his subjects will engage in the five basic moves which Goffman discusses: unwitting, naive, control, uncovering, and counter-uncovering moves. But in other circumstances where the investigator is able to unobtrusively view his subjects, only the unwitting and naive moves are involved.

For with participant observation there are situations where the subjects are unaware or unconcerned about being observed (i.e., engage in unwitting moves) and where the observer believes that the
subject can be taken as he appears (i.e., the observer is engaged in
what Goffman terms a naive move).

For instance, an investigation might be concerned with dating
behavior among teenagers from different ethnic backgrounds. More
specifically, the interest might be in hand-holding behavior, as one
aspect of what goes on when people date. Whereas the survey interviewer would have to rely on the respondents' willingness to report
or admit to holding hands with dating partners, the field investigator
could ask about and observe young people's behavior in a variety
of different settings. This might reveal, for example, that there are
strong normative proscriptions against young Italian males publicly
holding hands with their girl friends (Suttles, 1968), but that in other,
less public, situations they may do so. Especially with investigations of deviant behavior, such as drug use, where respondents may
be reluctant to admit such behaviors to the interviewer, the observer
is in a much better position for ascertaining the actual existence of
such actions. Advocates of observational studies have, of course,
long stressed these strengths of their methods.

As has been emphasized here, the methods of participant observation are in the anthropological tradition. They stand in contrast
to the methods of the great majority of sociological researchers
who have chosen to utilize procedures that appear to maximize
obtaining hard facts through the use of exact methods. Sometimes
these two traditions are characterized in terms of a quantitative
versus a qualitative approach. This seems to me a mistaken notion,
for all descriptions and analyses of behavior are inevitably *both*
qualitative and quantitative—although with observational studies
the counting and measurement may be implicit. For instance, in
observational studies there are assertions that a pattern of behavior
occurs *frequently, often, sometimes, seldom,* or in *many* different
situations. The issue is not whether one can more easily count or
measure with one procedure than with another, but rather whether
or not investigators are getting at the fullness and richness of the
phenomenon under study.

Whatever methods are used, however, it is obvious as Cicourel

(1964:39) states that, "researchers in the social sciences are faced with a unique methodological problem: the very conditions of their research constitute an important complex variable for what passes as the findings of the investigations." That some social scientists have recognized the extent to which their methods are themselves unknown features of the findings which their use generates has been shown by the recent work of Friedman (1967), Rosenberg (1969), Rosenthal (1966), and by this report as well. All of these works, however, have suggested ways of correcting or remedying flaws in various research techniques from within the same tradition which generated the problems in the first place. As Blum (1969:21) points out, most of these attempts to improve the validity of our measuring instruments accept people's "talk as an 'expression' of some underlying reality rather than as itself a practical accomplishment with socially organized features."

In response to this tendency, a number of sociologists influenced by the writing and teaching of Harold Garfinkel have turned to the task of inventing procedures for describing the methods employed by people for producing their talk as a socially situated and orderly course of activities. These "ethnomethodologists," as they call themselves, are heavily influenced by the phenomenologist Alfred Schutz. Ethnomethodology is seen as the investigation of the rational properties of everyday activities, and its concern is with finding out how individuals plan and explain their own behavior and how they determine what other persons are doing and saying. It is not so much a method as it is a way of locating, thinking about, and interpreting the phenomena of everyday life. In Garfinkel's (1967:vii) turgid prose, ethnomethodological studies are directed

> to the tasks of learning how members' actual, ordinary activities consist of methods to make practical actions, practical circumstances, common sense knowledge of social structures, and practical sociological reasoning analyzable; and of discovering the formal properties of commonplace, practical common sense actions, "from within" actual settings, as ongoing accomplishments of those settings.

What ethnomethodologists seem to be interested in, then, are those procedures which provide for people an understanding of themselves and each other. Or, put another way, Garfinkel and his associates are concerned with the principles that people utilize in the formulation of various practical judgments. Still another way of stating their interests is to say that those of the ethnomethodological persuasion are concerned with the methods by which people construct theories that allow them to engage in ordinary everyday activities.

While much of the writing of the ethnomethodological school is unclear and difficult to follow, the purpose of some of Garfinkel's (1967) empirical work seems clear in its intent. Research in which the investigator presents verbal or behavioral stimuli, not as an interviewer or a field observer, but as a member of the same social system, uncovers the responses that system members make to a violation or disturbance of normative expectations. It also, by forcing system members to try to restore order, exposes the members' methods and procedures for doing so; i.e., makes those methods observable and reportable.

Comparing the survey interview with observational techniques (including ethnomethodology), we see an important difference. In the typical interview situation, the interviewer's questions force the respondent to produce a number of behaviors (verbal reports) which the interviewer (or the investigator) treats as naturally oriented. The field observer, on the other hand, is more apt to observe relevant features which emerge from people's everyday activities and interactions. Some more radical observers (ethnomethodologists) would, upon locating relevant features concerning, say, rules of conduct, attempt to bring about various changes of such rules so as to assess the consequences of their alterations.

An excellent summary statement of the problems involved in comparing survey research with conventional field work and more radical observational studies is offered by Blum (1969:23):

The issue is how to produce rigorous and objective descriptions while preserving the theoretic character of the descriptions: each form of research tends to maximize its compliance with one of these conditions at the expense of the other. Thus, it is no trick to produce rigorous, relatively "behaviorized" descriptions of human activities (i.e., descriptions that can be reproduced by colleagues doing a minimum of interpretive work which draws upon knowledge extraneous to the event under study), but it *is* difficult to demonstrate the sensible character of such descriptions (i.e., the extent to which the descriptions are oriented to by members as constraints upon their activities and as possible products of those selfsame activities). Similarly, it is no feat to produce descriptions from "members" point of view (i.e., sensible and relevant descriptions) as long as such descriptions do not have to be reproduced with reference to observable affairs. The problem is one of creating sensible (theoretically relevant) descriptions that are objective (reproducible).

An attempt to deal with the problem of creating descriptions and analyses that get at the meaning of social actions and are, at the same time, reproducible and shareable with other sociologists constitutes one of the interests of the chapter that follows.

Chapter VII

Further Directions
in Sociological Research

Let me begin this final chapter by asserting that if sociologists are, as so many claim, really concerned with the meaning of social action, then the actor and his actions *cannot* be viewed wholly from the perspective of the outside, detached observer. This is true whether the subjective sociologist engages in the observation of behavior, utilizes interviews and questionnaires, examines available records and documents, employs various unobtrusive measures, or whatever. The study of social action has to be made, as much as possible, from the position of the actor. This being my view, the reader might ask: What of objectivity? Clearly, objectivity has the status of a sacred cow in all scientific endeavors, and it requires consideration here.

One of the most frequently encountered assertions in sociology is that *the researcher* (scientist, observer) must be *objective*. As Storer (1966) notes, objectivity is one of the norms of all science. Unfortunately, however, the exact meaning of the admonition to be objective is seldom made very clear. A definition in Webster's dictionary includes as central, "being without bias or prejudice; detached; impersonal." In sociology it is usually used to refer to the necessity for the scientist to collect, analyze, and interpret data in such a manner that he can completely separate his own values, beliefs, wishes, and preferences from the processes of data collection, analysis, and interpretation. Berelson and Steiner (1964:16) remark on this as follows: *"The data-collection is objective:* Once the investigation is under way, the investigator is bound to follow the data whatever way they may fall—for or against his hypothesis (however cherished), for or against his personal preferences as a man. Biased procedures in collecting data have no place in science, nor has biased perception of the results."* And Bierstedt (1963:17) states that: *"Objectivity* means that the conclusions arrived at as the result of inquiry and investigation are independent of the race, color, creed, occupation, nationality, religion, moral preference, and political predispositions of the investigator. If his research is truly objective, it is independent of any subjective elements, any personal desires, that he may have."

What they are saying is that the investigator should function independently of the reality he encounters: he should not influence (and should not be influenced by) the social worlds with which he comes into contact.[1] Ideally, then, repeated observations (measures, etc.) of a constant phenomenon by different investigators should yield similar results.

In other words, the investigator is expected to function as a data-collecting machine, and, theoretically at least, another machine would obtain the same results. Thus, whether the data-collecting machine is male or female, young or old, black or white, Jew or gentile, should not influence the results obtained. Nor should it matter whether the machine operates in one setting rather than another, whether the machine has certain expectations, needs, desires, or beliefs. For if it is really a good (objective) machine, the fact that it is an old, black female with a high need for approval should not lead to its collecting data (pertaining to the same constant phenomenon) that differ from those of another good machine which happens to be a young, white male with a low need for social approval.

---

[1] See, for instance, the recent book by Myrdal (1969) and the hysterical diatribe by Nisbet (1970).

How good are our machines? The answers seem obvious. Our machines are not very good; our data collectors are not very objective. This has been shown clearly in my review of some of the literature pertaining to bias and invalidity in Chapter II.

Since I have been arguing that sociological investigations based on survey interviews *are not* and *cannot be* objective, I will now consider the issue of objectivity in observational studies. The explanation which is sought in observational studies is sometimes framed as being different from that sought by the survey researcher That is, those in the *verstehen* tradition (as Sjoberg and Nett, 1968, put it) have as their goal understanding rather than prediction and explanation in the statistical sense discussed in Chapter I. However, there is no reason why the social researcher should not seek both types of explanation. For ultimately, both have to do with grasping and making sense of concrete social phenomena. And, in my view, this involves investigating, observing, and experiencing the *actual* social phenomena of interest whenever that is possible. One of the difficulties with the term *observational studies* is that, as Weick (1968:358–359) notes, the term is often used to

> refer to hypothesis-free inquiry, looking at events in natural surroundings, nonintervention by the researcher, unselective recording, and avoidance of manipulations in the independent variable. . . . It is proposed that hypothesis testing, partial contrivance of events, intervention, counting rather than rating, and selective recording can be just as much a part of observational methodology as their opposites *because they improve the observer's skill and understanding.*

Weick rejects, then, the traditional view of the observer as a passive bystander who unobtrusively obtains data with a minimum of involvement or intervention. As will become increasingly apparent in the remainder of this chapter, I too reject the traditional view of the uninvolved observer.

In a sense, survey researchers and participant observers alike make observations: *indirect,* in the case of survey researchers who rely upon the interpretations of informants (interviewers); *direct,* in the case of participant observers who witness or experience events or phenomena firsthand. The structured interview supposedly standardizes the observational process and this, its advocates argue, enhances reliability. But as Sjoberg and Nett (1968: 194–195) note, opponents of the structured interview see it "as over-simplifying or over-structuring reality: as imposing a spurious kind of order on the actor's 'world of meaning'." Those whose goal is understanding do not view knowledge as something out there which we can discover by being objective, but rather argue that knowledge is necessarily grounded in our personal involvement in common-sense practical activities. This means, as I have emphasized, that the observer must get at the meanings shared by any group members in whom he is interested.

There are, of course, some sociologists who would argue that there are no scientific procedures for getting at these meanings. This may be true. But if it is, then we must revise our conception of science rather than cease our attempts to get at meaning and achieve understanding. Those of a strict behaviorist persuasion argue that we can only know what we observe, and that we should not attribute any experience to those whom we study. Fortunately, not many sociologists subscribe to the doctrinaire behaviorist position. Most recognize that while we can observe only the manifest behavior of other persons (including individuals' reports of their behavior), we are constantly involved in making inferences as well. It seems obvious that our knowledge is almost always the result of both observation and inference, and not of observation alone. Whatever methodological views an investigator may have, he is bound to make certain assumptions and inferences that go beyond the data. For instance, Bakan (1967:80) quotes Tolman's statement of how to predict the behavior of rats: "But, in any case, I, in my future work, intend to go ahead imagining how, *if I were a rat,* I would behave as a result of such and such an appetite and such and such a degree of differentiation; and so on."

If, indeed, a psychologist studying rats is forced to make certain assumptions about what it is like to be a rat, we should acknowledge the obvious fact that no human being knows what it is to be a rat or any other animal. Similarly, when Konrad Lorenz (in Tinbergen, 1967:xiii) says that "it takes a very long period of watching to become really familiar with an animal and to attain a deeper understanding of its behavior . . . ," he is not content merely with observation (watching) but also has as a goal "under-standing." This poses for the investigator of animal behavior an insurmountable problem. He has no choice but to interpret animals' behavior in terms of the behavior of the human animal—as he views him. Fortunately, though, animals cannot be interviewed, nor can they fill out questionnaires. Thus, an investigator like Tinbergen (1967) who is interested in what he calls "Herring Gull Sociology," must study behavior *in situ*. In so doing, he is able to tell us a good deal about the herring gull and to demonstrate certain patterns of behavior, albeit *he* supplies the *meaning* of the herring gull's actions. For instance, Tinbergen (1967;137–138) states that: "the irrelevant behavior during aggressive encounters provided an outlet for strong impulses that were blocked because actual fighting was inhibited by the urge to escape." Again, to repeat the main point here, Tinbergen obviously does not know that the gull had, for instance, an "urge to escape." Rather, Tinbergen is providing an interpretation of certain behavior from the point of view of a scientist and human observer of animal behavior.

For the investigator of human behavior, the problem of inference is somewhat different. He does know what it is to be a human being, but he frequently assumes that we are all pretty much alike in certain important ways. That is, although the sociological researcher is interested in the extent to which people differ with regard to certain measures (independent and dependent variables), he often acts as if he possessed the knowledge necessary for making inferences about what people's words and actions mean. In other words, the sociological investigator interprets the data in terms of *his own experience*. It could not, of course, be otherwise. But it seems clear to me that in most instances his own experiences are not sufficiently relevant to provide an adequate basis for such interpretations. Still, the sociological researcher *must* concern himself with both behavior and experience. For as Laing reminds us, the participants in any social situation are influenced by both (Laing, 1967:25): "When two (or more) persons are in relation, the behavior of each towards the other is mediated by the experience of each of the other, and the experience of each is mediated by the behavior of each. . . . My experience of you is always mediated through your *behavior*."

The ultimate task of the sociological observer is to achieve what William James called "knowledge of" as contrasted with "knowledge about" certain social phenomena. To take a rather crude example, unless we have had a migraine headache, we are unlikely to have knowledge of this phenomenon although we may know about it. This does not mean that we are completely unable to understand something unless we have experienced it directly, but rather that whenever we can obtain such understanding we should try to do so. While people may be observed to work, talk, eat, sleep, etc., sociologists cannot be content with this type of observation. Their observations of behavior must be extended by inference to attributions about meaning and experience. As Laing et al. (1966:6) point out, we need to be concerned not only with the interaction and interexperience of one another's presence, but also with understanding the relation between each person's own experience and his own behavior—always within the context of the relationship between them.

If sociologists are to achieve this type of understanding, they cannot continue to place such a high emphasis on the narrowly conceived, mechanical notions of objectivity that I have described. For the task cannot be accomplished by cultivating a sense of consciousness cleansed of all subjective distortion, all personal involvement (Roszak, 1969). Unless the observer is involved with those in whom he is interested, he is apt to function as the unmoved spectator described by Maslow (1966:49):

> It means looking at something that is not you, not human, not personal, something independent of you the perceiver. . . . You the observer are, then, really alien to it, uncomprehending, and without sympathy or identification. . . . You look through the microscope or the telescope as through a keyhole, peering, peeping, from a distance, from outside, not as one who has a right to be in the room being peeped into.

OBSERVATION AND INVOLVEMENT

Problems of the observer's involvement in his investigations have been considered at length by several sociologists, including Gans (1968) who discusses three types of work roles for the sociological field worker. He emphasizes (1968:302–303) that at various times the field worker plays one or another of these roles: the *total participant* "who is completely involved emotionally in a social situation and who only after it is over becomes a researcher again and writes down what has happened"; the *researcher-participant* "who participates in a social situation but is personally only partially involved so that he can function as a researcher"; and the *total researcher* "who observes without any personal involvement in the situation under study." Gans notes that his own preference is for the "researcher-participant" role, arguing against the other two styles of field work. Certainly Gans's own work is among the very best in sociology at providing some of the understanding (knowledge of) which many sociologists demand. Furthermore, it is my view that his work is especially excellent in those situations where he was, even for a short time, a "total participant"—as, for example, when he had difficulty maintaining his own personal detachment when the city of Boston threatened to tear down the West End neighborhood as a slum (Gans, 1962).

Gans's preference, nevertheless, is for *avoiding* total involvement, and this is undoubtedly the preference of most other field workers as well. Gans also shares with the majority of other sociologists the view that the participant-observer cannot easily study his own people. In Gans's words (1968:304):

> He probably cannot work in a setting so close to his own life situation that he does share concerns and perspectives; for example, he could not study the department of sociology of which he is himself a member. Even if he were able to persuade his colleagues to treat him as a researcher rather than as a colleague, which is unlikely, it is doubtful that he could give up the temptation to participate, or to shed the feelings he had about his colleagues before he started to study them. Unless he is totally uninterested in his own department, he might want to act when he should observe, to like or dislike when he should research, and to argue when he should be listening.

It seems to me that Gans is saying that one cannot easily study his own people because (1) they are unwilling to treat him as a researcher rather than a colleague or one who is known in another capacity, and (2) one cannot be objective about the people he knows. But are these really necessary problems? Must they arise, and should they prevent us from studying people and situations that are already familiar to us?

I think it is true that our own people will not be apt to give us permission, and that we cannot be objective in studying them. With regard to the issue of objectivity, I have already stated my belief that it may prevent the achievement of understanding. As for permission, we do not necessarily require anyone else's permission. Novelists frequently write of situations and individuals with whom they are intimately familiar. This is probably more often the case than not. How objective they are is usually unknown. Certainly, however, the tumult that accompanied the novels of Thomas Wolfe or, more recently, Philip Roth, among others, suggests that some persons consider these works as improper and lacking in objectivity. That is, some consider the novelist who writes about his own people to be guilty of improprieties and of a biased viewpoint. That those who are written about can respond negatively, however, is clearly illustrated by Willie Morris's (1970:44) remarks concerning reactions to his book *North Toward Home*—a book describing himself and the people he grew up among in Yazoo, Mississippi:

> My book, as such things always do in our country, had deeply disturbed the town. Many people there thought I had damaged and condemned it. One person wrote me that I had besmirched the memory of my father. Another wrote a letter published on the front page of the *Yazoo Herald* that I had embarrassed my church, my school, and my friends. My mother received a few threatening calls. I got pointed warnings about what would happen if I came back.

While the novelist may become aware of the reactions of such people, it seems unlikely that he will be seriously affected by them in a significant way. They are not apt to be able to influence what he writes in the future, nor how other novelists and the book-buying public react to his works.

The situation of the sociologist who writes about other sociologists is quite different, for he is *dependent* upon the acceptance and good feelings of those about whom he writes. Should his fellow sociologists find his work improper and biased, he may pay a considerable price. While we do sometimes see articles by sociologists in which they describe their colleagues' behavior at conventions, for instance, we seldom see an analysis of one's colleagues' behavior in the department. In any case, names will not be mentioned. Yet many of us reacted very positively to Watson's (1968) recent book, *The Double Helix*. The acclaim and controversy that greeted the publication of Watson's book (and, in fact, the unwillingness of the Harvard University Press to publish it) is in dicative, I think, of just how unusual it is for a scientist to tell tales from within.

Thus, I am willing to grant that the sociologist cannot easily study his own department. However, this is not because of problems of permission and objectivity (as Gans suggests) but, rather, because of the fact that we are highly dependent upon those persons for our professional existence. This suggests, then, that there may be other situations where the sociologist cannot easily study his own people—probably family life is of this nature. Or, rather, the sociologist cannot let family or colleagues know that he is studying them, either by informing them of the fact or by explicitly writing about them. For almost as a necessary consequence of being a fellow human being, he studies them in one way or another.

If we consider the sociologist's own people from a different viewpoint, however, not as family and colleagues but as all those persons with whom he *can* become deeply involved and committed, then we can imagine a great variety of situations where the sociologist can function as a total participant. For instance, the work of Becker (1951) on jazz musicians and of Roth (1963) on tuberculosis patients is of that order. The studies of Festinger et al. (1956) and of Caudill (1958) are also of that nature, although I find the latter two studies objectionable on ethical grounds. But if the investigator plays a bona fide role (as did Becker and Roth) or informs that group that he is indeed studying them as did Whyte (1955), there should be no ethical conflict. In addition to these more-or-less formal investigations, it is possible for us to achieve understanding from consideration of many of our everyday, on-going, social involvements. Certainly, the work of Erving Goffman serves as a prime example of one sociologist's ability to get at the meaning embedded in many social situations and interactions. All of us are involved in a great variety of social activities that are open to sociological inquiry. Yet sociologists often fail to recognize that these are indeed fit subjects for investigation—even though, as I will spell out later, many of our theories and hypotheses come out of such experiences rather than from reviews of the literature, systematic thought, or other sources.

If we are to study behavior *in situ,* then, we must observe people in situations where they spend much of their time. To study such phenomena as conflict, conformity, jealousy, helping, anger, playing, or competition, we have to search for those situations in everyday life where these phenomena occur or where, with slight intervention, we might bring about their occurrence. In addition, we must be careful not to focus only on *verbal* behavior. Many observational studies, and most survey studies, seem to concentrate almost exclusively on vocal behavior, even though people spend only a small portion of their interactional time vocalizing. As Weick (1968:381) points out:

> It seems that the emphasis in our society on vocal performance, and the large amount of information that is stored in vocalized written words, has tempted investigators to conclude that man is essentially a vocalizing animal and, therefore, his words should be closely attended. Needless to say, it is tautological to state that because humans use language, language is the most important means of communication.

Thus in observational studies, sociologists must also concern themselves with the other classes of behavior discussed in Chapter III: nonverbal, spatial, and extra-linguistic behavior.

It is my view that observational methods are far better able than survey methods to get at these other types of behavior. With regard to this, one of the most obvious differences between observational and survey studies is that the survey interview is a strategy through which an investigator, in a sense, *produces* the phenomena of interest. He does this by asking respondents about conformity, or conflict, or status-seeking, or drug use, or whatever. It is not likely, therefore, that he will pay close attention to non-verbal kinds of behavior. In contrast, the investigator using observational techniques usually studies phenomena that he has not produced or brought about, although he may choose to try to do so in some instances. For the most part, he studies phenomena as they occur. Hence, he is apt to be far more sensitive to behavior other than that on the verbal level. A second major difference between the two research strategies is that the survey researcher usually imposes *in advance* categories or units of classification upon the behavior studied. Ideally, at least, this is much less the case in observational studies. Once again, this has implications for what the investigator's focus will be with regard to behavior.

Related to these two important differences between survey and observational studies is the issue of which method provides better understanding of some whole. Unfortunately, sociologists have not agreed upon criteria for deciding this question. It seems obvious that if the whole of interest to the investigator is a nation, it is unlikely that several observational studies can in some way be added up to provided knowledge of that particular whole. But it is equally unlikely that a series of survey studies can be accumulated so as to afford the desired knowledge. Nevertheless, it seems to me that in most instances we are better off with an adequate understanding of certain specific behaviors as we find them in everyday situations (or in small social systems) than with a vast amount of survey data concerning reports of behavior.

At present, of course, American sociologists place a disproportionately heavy emphasis on *atmostic* methods, where an attempt is made to derive sociological understanding and laws from studying an entity's parts. While such methods may be useful, as I indicated in Chapter V, in providing certain kinds of data, they cannot provide the type of understanding about the social world that I have described. However, we should not imagine that this is a problem peculiar to the study of social phenomena. Polanyi (1964:330) provides us with an example from the physical sciences:

We have a solid tangible inanimate object before us—let us say a grandfather clock. But we do not know what it is. Then let a team of physicists and chemists inspect the object. Let them be equipped with all the physics and chemistry ever to be known, but let their technological outlook be that of the stone age. Or, if we cannot disregard the practical incompatibility of these two assumptions, let us agree that in their investigations they shall not refer to any operational principles. They will describe the clock precisely in every particular, and in addition, will predict all its future configurations. Yet they will never be able to tell us that it is a clock. *The complete knowledge of a machine as an object tells us nothing about it as a machine.* . . . We identify a machine by understanding it technically; that is, by a participation in its purpose and an endorsement of its operational principles.

Similarly with sociology, our knowledge of the parts often distracts us from seeing what it is. As Robert Weiss (1968:343) has observed: "A methodology which requires us to search only for relationships among variables taken two at a time will find it difficult to make understandable such entities. This more analytic course may well lead to important generalizations, but it will leave unexplained the fundamental characteristic of living systems, their organizations." If we are to go beyond the accumulation of lists in which two variables (or several variables, in the case of multivariate and path analysis) bear a certain relation to one another (and, as we already know, this usually means a very weak relationship) to a concern with *how a system works*, we must enter into it more frequently than most of us do at present. Such participation is necessary to provide us with reactions of our own which will help us to properly understand the reports and behavior of others. For only by becoming involved in what we are studying can we fix upon the thing itself, become aware of it, experience it, and obtain "knowledge of" as well as "knowledge about" it. Certainly if we sociologists are really interested in process and interaction, as we so often claim, and if we wish to study the construction of meanings and of social relations, we can only do so from more active involvement and participation.

Ideally, perhaps, the sociologist would have at his disposal highly objective methods for determining social meanings that did not involve personal participation and involvement as crucial features. Since we do not have such methods, we are, as Douglas (1970) points out, highly dependent upon our own experiences in society for our basic understanding of society. This point has, of course, been long recognized by many sociologists, beginning perhaps with Dilthey and Weber (Hughes, 1961). There is, then, for those who reject an objective interpretation of human events a distinctive methodological feature. In the words of Tiryakian (1965: 678), who has discussed this issue at length, "since the observer is a human being studying other human beings, he has access to the inner world of experience. This direct access is 'sympathetic understanding' and 'intuition' by means of which the observer can view cultural phenomena 'from within'."

In my view, however, "sympathetic understanding" and "intuition" are not enough. For, whenever possible, direct involvement is much more likely to provide us with the subjective meanings in which we are interested. Obviously, the social meanings of actions to various actors will not be revealed simply by our becoming involved, for total involvement (going native, becoming too involved) on a permanent basis necessarily makes these meanings inaccessible. Douglas (1970:199–200) states that:

> the solution lies in adopting alternating stances while maintaining one's ultimate (or latent) identity as a sociologist. A sociologist who "goes native," or becomes totally involved as a member in the group he is studying, can be of immense value to us by telling us how it looks from the inside; but he can only do this if he returns to being a sociologist and if he retains a true meaning of the experience. . . . In short, the problems involved in managing personal involvement so as to get at the social meanings *and* be able effectively to communicate them are solvable; but the problems of unravelling the social meanings in experience seem insoluble without a high degree of personal involvement.

What Douglas stresses is the need for studies of everyday situations in everyday life. Theoretical ideas (or assumptions, beliefs, theories) that we already have can be evaluated by using them to predict the outcome of *our own* and other people's activities in various social situations. That is, we can test some of our theories about social phenomena by acting (or refraining from acting) in a certain way and seeing what happens. Now, obviously, how we define what happens is dependent on the meaning of an actor's behavior. The usual assumption in sociological research is that any fool who knows how to be objective can see what happens and convey this to the rest of us. But we have already seen that this is not the case at all—at least in survey studies. Is the participating observer any better off?

For one thing, it would seem that what is immediately experienced by a participating member of a society is different from what is experienced by the objective nonparticipant. But since objective nonparticipants are so unsuccessful in agreeing as to exactly what was experienced, what happened, what was meant, perhaps we should give greater attention to the participant's experiences. After all, in most everyday activities we (both as sociologists and as societal members) consider that which we have immediately experienced ourselves as being more accurate than that which we have not experienced in the same immediate sense. As Douglas (1970:217) points out: "It is precisely the criteria of the immediate experience of the observer that the phenomenologist or existentialist is using when he insists on studying the phenomena 'on their own terms'."

Since Weber (1949) and Mannheim (1957), more and more sociologists have come to recognize that there is a differential distribution of realities within any society. That is, there are *multiple realities*—consisting of information believed by somebody to represent facts about the social world—which are differentially allocated to people by virtue of their location in society (Holzner, 1968). Mannheim (1957:219) recognized this when he stated that "the greater art of the sociologist consists in his attempt always to relate changes in mental attitudes to changes in social situations." From this perspective, the reality within which members of society conduct their lives is, to a large extent, of their own construction (Berger and Luckmann, 1966). Therefore, we can often best grasp the realities which constitute other people's definitions of the situation by placing ourselves in that situation. As Greer (1969:167–168) notes:

One of the major ways of exploring social situations is through interacting with the protagonists. Whether one is a participant observer or an observing participant, his chances of intuiting the rationale of behavior are increased by playing a part in the game. Through his imaginings of the imagination of others, he gains awareness of their expectations, learning like any participant, but analyzing in another frame of reference.

In arguing that social action cannot be comprehended without reference to the motivation of actors, and to the meanings *they* impute to their actions, I obviously assume that this meaning *can be* revealed and communicated to others. Schutz (1954;267) points to how one can understand the meaning of other persons' actions when he states:

To a certain extent, sufficient for many practical purposes, I understand their behavior, if I understand their motives, goals, choices, and plans originating in *their* biographically determined circumstances. Yet only in particular situations, and then only fragmentarily, can I experience the others' motives, goals, etc.—briefly, the subjective meanings they bestow upon their actions, in their uniqueness. I can, however, experience them in their typicality.

This is possible, says Schutz, because—to varying extents—men share the same intersubjective world.

In emphasizing typification, those in the phenomenological tradition are suggesting that investigators—like other individuals—comprehend both actors and action through the typifications or types which their models create. Weber (1949:90) wrote of these "ideal types" as follows:

An ideal type is formed by the one-sided *accentuation* of one or more points of view and by the synthesis of a great many diffuse, discrete, more or less present and occasionally absent *concrete individual* phenomena, which are arranged according to those one-sidedly emphasized viewpoints into a unified *analytical* construct. . . . In its conceptual purity, this mental construct . . . cannot be found empirically anywhere in reality. It is a *utopia*.

The individual who exemplifies one or another ideal type is, of course, a methodological phantom. But men *like* that can be located (Nathanson, 1970). An investigator constructs these ideal types out of his knowledge, experience, and familiarity with those whose actions concern him. Nathanson discusses, for example, the historian's construction of a "typical wine merchant in Jerusalem in the first century, A.D." He notes (Nathanson, 1970:93) that:

> the author of a "Daily Life" study has done his job well if he gives us the merchant as an "ideal type," as a construction built out of hundreds of descriptions, reports, documents, letters, diaries, and indirectly out of a much larger and more profound study of the macrocosmic history of the times, including its literature, its art, its science and technology, and its philosophical and religious foundations.

Similarly, the sociologist interested in everyday social behavior must, in some sense, share in the lives of those whom he investigates. This means that in order to establish the meaning of an action, the investigator must rely on his grasp of the common-sense *understandings* shared by the participants in the interaction itself— not on a body of common-sense knowledge shared with his colleagues (Wilson, 1970).[2]

PERSONAL KNOWLEDGE

Up to this point, I have been considering how the sociologist gathers his data. I want now to consider this problem from a some-

[2] The methodological implications of a concern with understanding the meanings of men's actions have long been recognized (Blumer, 1954, 1956, 1962, 1966; Mills, 1940b), and have been discussed with great care and insight by Aaron Cicourel in his important book, *Method and Measurement in Sociology* (1964). Still, it seems to be business as usual within the sociological profession. At the very same time that many sociologists are asking blacks in our society to "tell it like it is," the majority of sociologists continue to proceed in their data-collection activities as if it were fully understood what "it is" in most other areas of sociological inquiry.

what different perspective. What I am going to suggest is that sociologists should give more serious consideration to those data which they have gathered "in their heads" as direct participants in a great variety of social activities and situations. In that all discussions of sociological research regard data gathering in terms of *purposive* scientific investigations, their concern is with going out to collect data. However, there is another way of regarding the gathering of sociological data. In considering this, I will, first, discuss some suggestions made by the psychologist David Bakan. Then, I will offer a personal example of how one might utilize personal knowledge of certain social phenomena.

In a provocative paper entitled "A Reconsideration of the Problems of Introspection," David Bakan (1967) notes that the method of introspection fell into general disrepute with the inception and growth of behaviorism in America, and that most social scientists still consider it an inappropriate method for achieving understanding. The major criticism against the method of introspection has been that its data are not public as in the case of overt behavior, where, at least theoretically, two or more persons can observe a given phenomenon simultaneously. Bakan acknowledges that introspection generates data which are not public in that sense, but questions the value of the "criterion of publicity" as it is called. He argues that a more important consideration is the publicity not of the data, but of the report. Bakan (1967:99) puts it this way:

Even though the process of introspective observation is, in a sense, private, the information gleaned from the observation must be public. This raises the question of language and communication. There are two questions that may be asked in connection with language with respect to introspection: First, if we relate our introspections to one another, would we understand one another? Second, if we do understand one another, how does this come to pass? If the answer to the first question is to any degree affirmative, then to that extent is the criterion of publicity of report satisfied. For the answer to the first question we appeal, at the very least, to common sense. If we hear a person say, "I am sorry," or "I am worried," or "I feel sick," etc., there is hardly any question what he means. . . . The answer to the second question now becomes a matter for empirical investigation.

Bakan (1967:103–104) goes on to describe a procedure which involved his sitting at a typewriter and typing whatever came to mind regarding a particular topic: in this case, retention and revelation of secrets. He reports that he attempted to write as if the material would never be released (made available to others). Through this kind of writing, which represents an oscillation between a mood of free expression and an analytic mood, with the free expression being the subject of the analysis, he arrived at a set of a dozen propositions concerning secrecy. An example is (Bakan, 1967:104): "We are more prone to confess a guilty secret when we can believe that others have the same secret guilt. . . ."

What Bakan attempts through this method of introspection, then, is to, in a sense, maximize his ability to uncover various kinds of information which he has collected during his lifetime—both as a psychologist and as a human being. To Bakan, one of the merits of this kind of approach is that it studies the phenomenon of psychological interest *directly,* which is seldom the case in most psychological, or other social science, investigations. He says that (Bakan, 1967:108–109), "the method has a directness not to be found in any other method of investigation of psychological phenomena. In any investigation each thing lying between the phenomenon and the data is a source of error. These sources of error are minimized by the method being proposed."

Obviously Bakan cannot ignore the matter of the validity of findings derived from introspective investigations. And he does consider the problem at some length. While I do not find his arguments completely persuasive, I do not see that problems of validation with the methods of introspection are necessarily more difficult than with other procedures. Let me now proceed to offer a personal example of how sociologists might make more explicit use of some of the data in their heads.

For several years, I have been playing touch football with some other football fanatics on Sunday mornings. During three years at Dartmouth and four years in New York City, I have continued this activity. At one time or another, those playing have included: students (graduate and undergraduate), faculty from a variety of disciplines, doctors, lawyers, businessmen, schoolteachers, salesmen, and a number of others whose occupations I never learned. As far as I can tell, the fact that I am a sociologist has been of absolutely no consequence in these games. That is, whether one is a sociologist, a lawyer, or a dock worker is completely irrelevant to those playing the game and to the manner in which the game is played.

Imagine that now, after having participated in such games over a period of several years, I should become interested *as a sociologist* in finding out what it means to be a weekend touch-football player, i.e., what the behavior means to the actors in the situation. It is my view that should I seriously reflect upon what the game means to me as a player, my understanding will be far superior to what would have been obtained had I entered into the game *for the purpose* of finding out what the games mean to the participants. For my total involvement in the games has been as a member of that social system—not as a sociologist. I believe that my knowledge of the perspectives and experiences of the players is of a different order from that of the sociologist who goes to *study* the players. That is, I am better able to locate the taken-for-granted *rules* involved in playing the game. Obviously, I am still able to do what any social researcher might do: interview others (players), observe the players, etc. But by participating *as a player* I have acquired *personal knowledge* of what it means to participate in the social activity of playing touch football. Such knowledge could not have been acquired had I accepted the ideals of scientific detachment and objectivity. This does not mean, of course, that all, or even most, areas of sociological interest are equally amenable to the acquisition of personal knowledge. But there are a wide variety of activities, situations, and events in which each of us has participated that are open to such inquiry.

Sociologists should explicitly utilize such personal experiences, not deny them. They must concern themselves less with obtaining new observations and more with interpreting the meaning of what they have already experienced. As Gouldner (1970:482) so correctly asserts: "For surely men may be led to truth no less than to falsehood by their socially shaped personal experiences in the world.

Indeed, there is no other way in which they can approach truth. Surely truth, no less than error, must be born of social experience."

A CONSIDERATION OF RULES

One problem for the sociologist utilizing either traditional forms of participant observation or the kinds of personal involvement discussed earlier in studying action (behavior which is meaningful to the actor) is how to achieve understanding. This is, however, only one of the problems involved in such investigations, for there are two others of considerable magnitude. The first is how to communicate in such a manner that other sociologists will indeed know or recognize that the investigator has achieved the understanding which he seeks. The second is how to make his findings shareable with others. That is, the observer must produce sensible descriptions that are in some way reproducible or replicable by other observers. Weber (1947:90) recognized this when he wrote that "all interpretation of meanings, like all scientific observation, strives for clarity and verifiable accuracy in insight and comprehension."

Let me consider these two issues, one at a time, beginning with the problem of how to demonstrate that one has achieved understanding. Recall that I have argued that sociologists are able to understand people's behavior if they understand their motives, goals, choices, and plans. The sociologist's task, then, is to understand what the social world (or some portion thereof) means to the observed actor or actors. But what is it to understand something, to grasp the sense of something? That is, what is the criterion for understanding?

One answer is that actions can be viewed as done for reasons which involve the *following of rules*. For a characteristic that distinguishes human beings from other organisms is that humans follow rules. Thus, one criterion for understanding is the demonstration that we have located the *rules* which people are following in various activities. In trying to locate such rules, we must, of course, take into account not only the actions of one or another actor whose behavior is in question but also the *reactions of other people* to what he does. Therefore, it is important, as Birdwhistell

(1969) has pointed out, in trying to grasp the rules of interaction that those being observed not be observed in isolation from other members of the same culture or subculture. That is, the investigator needs to have access to at least one other member who is also looking at the interaction in question, so that he can see how he responds to the interaction in question. Otherwise, the investigator has no basis for judgment as to whether the behavior being observed is usual or customary, i.e., whether or not it follows some cultural rules. As Winch (1967:30) observes: "It is only in a situation in which it makes sense to suppose that somebody else could in principle discover the rule that I am following that I can intelligibly be said to follow a rule at all."

What is important, then, is that in principle it be possible for other individuals to grasp a rule and judge whether it is being correctly followed. This is true in that people's inward standards of behavior are derived from experience in human society with its socially established rules. As has been emphasized throughout this book, the individual in his interactions with another must take into account what the other is up to; he must have some theories or notions about how the other is likely to behave, how the other will respond to his actions, and the like. In a sense, both actors must *know the rules,* for all social activities are rule ridden. The extent to which people act in accordance with rules is well illustrated by Moore and Anderson (1965:73):

> Consider the following problem. Suppose you were to find yourself on a lifeless moon, with no possibility of returning to, or communicating with, the earth. Suppose also that you were in a frame of mind to do something bad. What would you do? In informal conversation, this question has elicited a wide variety of initial responses, but after a little thought the answer generally settles on the following point: the only way to do something bad in the circumstances is to break some *rule.* . . . The "conclusion" seems to us inescapable that *self-consciously acting in accordance with a rule* (or formulating such rule) is one of the fundamental aspects of social interaction.

Let us consider the matter of rules somewhat further. If we should say that "X helped Y because they are friends," we are really asserting that the notion of friendship involves conducting oneself according to certain *rules*. One of the sociologist's major tasks is to formulate these rules. But, in addition, the force of an explanation is dependent on the fact that the concepts used by the sociologist in his explanation must be grasped not only by other sociologists but by X himself. For X must have some idea of what it is to be "friends" and of a connection between this and the idea of "helping" someone (Winch, 1967). Thus the terms of an explanation must be familiar to the observed (subjects, respondents, whatever) as well as to the observer. This does not mean that the abstract theoretical language used by the sociologist must be familiar to both the subject and the investigator, but rather that it must be possible to ultimately use a language familiar to both. Consider, as another instance, an example offered by Kaufman (1958:162), where the concern is to understand the meaning of several individuals sitting around manipulating small pieces of cardboard in what is called a card game:

> The players form a society by engaging in a social activity that implies observation of certain rules, namely, the rules of the game. Each player pursues his own ends, which run counter to the ends of at least one other player and are more or less determined by the rules of the game and by the given situation (distribution of the cards, etc.). Consequently, an observer can explain, and, to a certain extent, predict, the behavior of the players in terms of the rules of the game. Every card game is thus a field of application of rules.

Again, I emphasize that this explanation must be in terms familiar to both the analyst and, in this case, the players in the card game.

If a sociologist is to begin to understand (i.e., grasp the rules) what he is investigating, he must have some feeling for that which he studies. Even when he uses his own (sociological) concepts, these technical terms require, as I have noted previously, some *previous understanding* of those other concepts which belong to the activities under investigation. This means, for example, that a sociologist who wishes to explain the nature and consequences of certain kinds of behavior may wish to use such a technical concept as "social class." Now, the term is not generally used by laymen in their everyday conversations. But it can be tied logically to concepts which do exist in everyday activities, for the use of, say, "lower class" by the sociologist presupposes his understanding of what it means to have little education, be poor, unemployed, and so on. This suggests that to understand lower-class individuals' behavior, we must familiarize ourselves with the concepts in terms of which *they* view their situation. That is, we must become aware of the rules which specify for them the relevant features of their situation. It is not open to the investigator to arbitrarily impose his own standards from without.

As should be clear from the above, the sociologist concerned with interpretive understanding must also utilize careful observation. Unfortunately, Max Weber, whose genius it was to emphasize the importance of interpretive understanding, was very unclear in his account of how to ascertain the validity of suggested sociological interpretations. Weber seemed to believe that the appropriate procedure for verifying a hypothesis was to establish statistical regularities based on observations (that is, the collection of data). It seems obvious that statistical laws or regularities have nothing to do with the correctness of an interpretation. If a proffered interpretation does not verify the hypothesis, statistics are not the ultimate criteria for determining the validity of sociological interpretation as Weber seems to suggest. An interpretation disproving the hypothesis may require a better interpretation, not something different in kind. As Peter Winch (1967:115) points out:

> The difference is precisely analogous to that between being able to formulate statistical laws about the likely occurrences of words in a language and being able to understand what was being *said* by someone who spoke the language. . . . "Understanding," in situations like this, is grasping the *point* or *meaning* of what is being done or said.

Thus, the compatability of an interpretation with a statistical pattern or association does not serve as evidence of its validity. Rather, the objective meaning of acoustic or visual phenomena is the meaning attributed to those signs by a rule generally accepted according to a given scheme of interpretation *within a social group.*

Consider, now, the second problem referred to above: how to make our findings shareable. Speaking of this "norm of publicity," Greer (1969:7) points out that: "individuals' operations, whether they are speculative and logical, or empirically descriptive, must be open to group surveillance—a jury of one's peers."

How, then, can we accomplish this? I have already stated my belief that the sociological investigator must take account of his relation to the phenomena which he investigates. But he must also take account of another relation, that to his fellow sociologists. The investigator has to be sensitive to certain *procedural rules* governing the investigation itself. Recognizing that science can be defined in terms of consensus about rules of procedure, we have to conclude that these rules too must be made explicit by the investigator. Whatever social phenomena an investigator studies, he observes certain facts about them. Clearly, though, to do so presupposes that he is already capable of communicating with other sociologists about what he is doing, i.e., that he is following some procedural rules that are in principle intelligible to fellow sociologists.

Let us consider this problem in light of the following. Glaser and Strauss (1965:7) note that the "fieldworker knows *that* he knows, not only because he's there in the field and because of his careful verification of hypotheses, but because 'in his bones' he feels the worth of his final analysis." The issue, then, is this. How can someone else share what is known by Glaser and Strauss or other sociological researchers? How can we ensure public verifiability?

There are no easy answers to these questions. However, I can certainly provide tentative answers. What is necessary is that the participating observer be able to provide other potential participating observers (in this case, other sociologists) with a set of explicit *instructions* (which are at present taken for granted) on how to put themselves in the same situation so as to have the same or similar experiences.[3] Obviously, this is what we have to do anyhow in sociology when we collect data through survey interviews. The principal difference is that, at present, data collectors are told to remain objective so that personal factors will not affect either the data or the results of their investigations, and they furthermore have operated with a certain set of instructions which involve the use of interview schedules in survey research.

In other words, the present dominant paradigm in sociology contains the assumption that if we just "program" our data collectors correctly they can achieve objectivity and can provide the instructions for other data collectors to obtain similar results: "Go to the house, knock on the door, tell the respondent that this is a scientific study, that his cooperation will be appreciated, that there are no right or wrong answers; read the questions in the following order, don't let your own feelings influence the responses," and so forth.[4]

Supposedly, at least, several dozen interviewers can be programmed in the same manner with adequate instructions provided for all. While this is the goal, we have seen that we do not even come close to achieving it. For to provide the same instructions would really mean that we should not exclude anything which makes a difference in people's responses. As far as most survey researchers are concerned, of course, interviewers of different sexes, ages, races, and social class backgrounds can collect data in different settings, at different times, and will still be doing the same thing in following the instructions.

Conducting interviews with 500 respondents actually involves 500 (or 499) replications of the same investigation. And, as has been documented earlier, they do not meet the usual standards of replicability. For when the data-collection procedures (including

[3] This is not, of course, a guaranteed cure-all, for as Bramson (1961:151) points out: "Intersubjectively confirmable truth can still be subject to the limitations of collective ignorance. Thus in the time of Ptolemy, the consensus of the competent was that the sun rotated around the earth. But there appears to be no way of avoiding this problem, except to make provision for continuity of inquiry, leaving the door open for new approaches."

[4] Reiss (1968:358) remarks: "Some suggest that surveys are more standardized, though the history of surveys argues quite to the contrary. What is clear is that in the history of the survey we have developed more systematic procedures for dealing with bias though . . . we rarely employ most of them."

all response-relevant variables in the context of the interview) are not controlled, not reported, and so not replicated, the data remain unverifiable by others.[5] In addition, and partially as a consequence of the same factors, the data are frequently invalid as well. Despite the fact that they are not easily verified, interviews still continue as the dominant technique for collecting data about social phenomena.

One reason for this is that most sociologists apparently assume that it is virtually impossible to replicate observational studies, while the replication of survey studies is seen as much more easily accomplished. In fact, though, survey studies are seldom replicated. Not only are the data collectors different in studies that claim to be replications of previous investigations (that is, they do not possess the same characteristics in the same mixes), but the measures employed are seldom comparable. As was noted in Chapter I, it is as if each researcher started over in developing measures of various social phenomena. There are very few sociological studies that come close to meeting the scientific criteria for replication.

Studies based on personal involvement or participation are also seldom replicated. So it is difficult to estimate just how many problems are involved in their replication. Among the main reasons for this lack of replication is the fact that to become deeply enough involved in a group so as to understand it is extremely time-consuming, strenuous, and tense work (Gans, 1968). Certainly, the work of Whyte (1955), Gans (1962, 1967), Dalton (1959), and Liebow (1968)—to point to several sociological studies where the researchers have become highly involved insiders—all represent a considerable commitment of time and self to the investigations. However, it is not only these difficulties that have stood in the way of replication of studies involving personal involvement. Douglas (1970:220) lists some other basic reasons:

(1) natural situations and observers are both very complicated and necessarily "meet" each other in very compli-

---

[5] Despite the shortcomings of such data, they constitute the vast bulk of the evidence cited by Berelson and Steiner in their book, *Human Behavior: An Inventory of Scientific Findings.* They note (Berelson and Steiner, 1964:27): "But since in this book we limit ourselves to what is more or less proved *[sic]* about human behavior, we shall bring in the results of case studies only when they have been verified in some way." Thus, Whyte is cited once, and Gans, Becker, Goffman, Dalton, and C. Wright Mills are completely ignored.

cated ways that lead to the development of (historical) concrete meaningful relations which are very hard to record, and harder to replicate; (2) natural observations necessarily involve a minimum of control, so it would be exceedingly difficult to control these complexities; and (3) situations and groups necessarily change a great deal, so it would be hard to study the "same" situation or group.

These are all problems of some magnitude. But they are essentially the same problems that exist with respect to survey research, although many assume that they have been solved for survey studies. Whatever means one chooses to gather his data, such problems are not easily dealt with. Still, it is important to suggest some procedures for dealing with problems of replicability in observational studies. One thing that we should do, as Douglas (1970) suggests, is to provide checks on the research process itself. What he means by this is that researchers should, as far as possible, provide us with highly detailed accounts of how they went about conducting their research, how their experiences or observations were gotten in the research situation. As Douglas (1970:222) points out: "The simple expedient of insisting on more publication of the *actual,* as opposed to idealized or reconstructed, procedures followed would help a great deal."

THEORIES, METHODS, AND THE INVESTIGATOR'S EXPERIENCE

While Douglas's suggestions have considerable merit, I believe that sociologists must go further if they are to allow for the replicability of observational methods. To indicate the direction in which I feel we must go, I will develop further two of the themes set forth earlier in this book.

The first concerns the "vicious circle" quality of the relationship between theories and methods: *what we know about social behavior is dependent on our methods for studying behavior, while our methods for studying social behavior are dependent upon what we know about it.* Thus, the extreme reliance upon interviews and questionnaires by sociological researchers assumes that we know certain things about people and their behavior. At the very least, their utilization assumes that there is a socially shared system of symbols and their meanings, and that the meanings conveyed by linguistic and nonlinguistic behaviors (signs given and given-off) are clear and agreed upon by most societal members.

Yet Cicourel (1964) and Deutscher (1966, 1968, 1969), among others, have raised questions about linguistic comparability. Deutscher (1968:319) remarks on this:

> We are confronted with many serious problems in the methodological domain, but what is perhaps the most devastating gap is our unwillingness (and consequent inability) to come to grips with semantics: What do people intend to convey when they answer our questions, or, for that matter, when they speak at all? What do people understand to be the intent and meaning of our questions?

The point here is that we usually ignore such questions, choosing our methods on the basis of some implicit model of the actor, a model which, unfortunately, is never fully described and made explicit by most researchers. The failure to recognize this is, in my view, an important failure on the part of most sociologists.

There is, of course, a further, and related, failure of vision among most sociological researchers. A concern with that constitutes a second theme of this book: *the unwillingness to recognize that the source of most sociological knowledge about social behavior is the behavior involved in the process of collecting data.* This has been discussed in the previous chapters mainly in terms of various biases which are involved in the data-collection process. Attention has been given to ways of minimizing systematic biases in survey studies, and other alternate procedures for collecting data have been discussed. An obvious question suggests itself from that earlier discussion. Is it possible to develop "artifact-free" measures? My answer to this query is a clear and resounding *no*. As long as sociologists gather their data through research methods involving human investigators, their presence will always influence the results to some extent. The reason for this has been emphasized throughout this report: the same social processes involved in other social encounters are bound to occur in sociological research. In recognizing the existence of these processes in the laboratory experiment, Friedman (1967:xi) has suggested that "individualistic, intrapersonal, monadic, natural science perspectives on the psychological experiment and psychology need to be supplemented by interactional, interpersonal, dyadic, social science perspectives."

But merely taking a different perspective, as Friedman suggests, is not necessarily going to improve our methodological procedures. For whatever perspective the researcher employs, his own implicit theories and models of the actor will determine his methods for collecting data about social phenomena. They will determine not only how he collects his data, but of equal importance; what he sees as data, the way he constructs questions, the manner by which he codes his materials, and the way he interprets them (Cicourel, 1964). Thus, social investigators *must make an effort to communicate, as part of their presentation of a study, information concerning the theories and assumptions about social behavior that guided their research.* Related to this is a need for them to be more explicit about the context and grounds for their question constructions, coding procedures, and so on.

It is about time that sociologists began to recognize and to admit to the influence of their own points of view on what they see and how they see it. In recent years historians appear to have been more sensitive than sociologists to the effects of their own involvement on the realities they study (Lynd, 1968). Many writers have begun to recognize and make explicit the personal nature of their writings. Younger novelists and journalists, especially, are less and less willing to employ an omniscient narrator speaking in the third person. Consequently, we see such excellent samples of personal journalism as the writings of Norman Mailer (1968), Jimmy Breslin (1969), and Jack Newfield (1970), and the fine autobiographical fiction of Kurt Vonnegut (1969) and Frederick Exley (1969).

Even that great bastion of respectability, the *New York Times*, has been involved in controversy concerning its objectivity. I refer not to the attacks on the press by Vice-President Agnew, but rather to conflict among the *Times'* staff itself. As Talese (1970:72–73) writes:

> The Times in principle tried to be objective in its news coverage, but in reality it could not always be. It was run by hu-

mans, flawed figures, men who saw things as they *could* see them, or sometimes *wished* to see them; interpreting principles to suit contemporary pressures, they wanted it both ways; it was the oldest story of all. Ideally, *The Times* desired no opinions within its news columns, restricting opinion to its editorial page. Realistically, this was not possible. The editors' opinions and tastes were imposed every day within the news—either by the space they allowed for a certain story or the position they assigned it, or printed for only one edition, or edited heavily, or held out for a few days. . . . The reporter's ego was also a factor in the news coverage—he wrote what he wrote best, he wrote what he understood, reflecting the total experience of his lifetime, shades of his pride and prejudice.

And J. Anthony Lukas, the *Times'* correspondent and Pulitzer Prize winner who covered the Chicago Seven trial, complained that the demands of objectivity imposed on him by the *Times'* editors made it (quoted in Diamond, 1970:43) "very difficult to give a true picture of what is happening in the courtroom."[6]

It seems apparent, then, that at least some social science practitioners and professional writers are coming to recognize that objectivity cannot simply be taken for granted. Nor, in my view, are they likely to continue to accept admonitions that they try to *remove* their influence on those they are studying or *remove* themselves from their writings—for such contamination is inevitable. Rather than remove their influence, they must come to *recognize* it. This means that they must strive to know themselves and to recognize what they bring with them to their research and writings. With regard to the sociologist, it seems clear to me that even the most abstract of sociological theories and even the most scientific of sociological methods are highly dependent upon the sociologist's own experiences in the society which surrounds him.

My view that the sociologist's own experiences are involved in—and, as I shall point out, give rise to—the theories and methods which he employs is a radically different view from the one held by

[6] For some other, less explicit illustrations of correspondents' own viewpoints and interests influencing their writings, see the articles from "Times Talk"—the house organ of *The New York Times*—contained in Adler (1970).

such sociologists as Merton (1957:86–87), for instance, who sees theory and methodology as distinct specialties, separated from everyday matters.

At the outset we should distinguish clearly between sociological theory, which has for its subject matter certain aspects and results of the interaction of men and is therefore substantive, and methodology, or the logic of scientific procedure. The problems of methodology transcend those found in any one discipline, dealing either with those common to groups of disciplines or, in more general form, with those common to all scientific inquiry. Methodology is not peculiarly bound up with sociological problems, and, though there is a plenitude of methodological discussions in books and journals of sociology, they are not thereby rendered sociological in character. Sociologists in company with all others who essay scientific work, must be methodologically wise; they must be aware of the design of investigation, the nature of inference, the requirements of a theoretic system. But such knowledge does not contain or imply the particular *content* of sociological theory. There is, in short, a clear and decisive difference between *knowing how to test* a battery of hypotheses, and *knowing the theory* from which to derive hypotheses to be tested.

Merton has been quoted at length here because it is important to see the extent to which Merton views theory and methodology as completely separate involvements within sociology. For Merton tells us, and I think his view is shared by most sociologists, that the methodologist not only is not a theorist but that he need not be a researcher. That is, the methodologist's concern is with knowing how to test hypotheses and, supposedly, he can know how without actually having to engage in research. In fact, Richard Hill (1969:27) has suggested that there is a growing separation between research and methodology. Hill (1969:28) criticizes this separation, as well as what he sees as a separation between theory and research, stating: "Within sociology, methodological developments ought to be judged in terms of their contribution to the solution of the theoretical and substantive problems of the discipline rather than in terms of their abstract elegance." I agree fully with Hill's views regarding the "general methodologist," and I share his hope that this category will soon become, in his words, "a null class."

While agreeing with Hill that there is an analytic distinction in the trichotomy—theorist, methodologist, researcher—I do not see the distinction in the same way that he does. That is, I recognize that the following may be true: theorists may not possess the explicit skills for knowing how to test hypotheses, and they may not engage in empirical research; methodologists may not have a particular interest in the content of sociological theory, and may not undertake research; and researchers may not have as a special interest either the content of theory or knowing how to test hypotheses. But I firmly believe that in the world of realities the situation is otherwise. As I have stressed earlier, researchers *do* employ theories. And it is inconceivable to me that general methodologists as well do not employ various theories in their work—even if they deal with such interests as Markov chains, computer simulation, or game theory. Even the theorist utilizes various methods for testing some of his ideas about the world around him.

Whatever method the sociologist employs to collect his data, he is always functioning as a theorist, trying to make sense out of whatever he observes. This is a consequence not of his being a social scientist, but is rather a normal activity of everyday life for all persons. Gillin (1954:258) states this point:

Every "normal" human being is, willy-nilly, a theorizer. This is merely to say that no normally intelligent member of the species Homo sapiens (with an I.Q. of, say, 90 or above) can look at anything without formulating a theory (or following some traditional formulation) about what he observes. To take a very trivial example, Joe Doakes hammers a nail into a board and the nail crumples. Doakes says to himself (if he has no audience) "That must be hard wood instead of soft wood." That statement of Doakes is a theoretical conclusion or theorem from certain implicit postulates. It is meant to explain the result he had from trying to drive the nail. Furthermore, it is a verifiable theorem. There are certain methods available to Doakes to determine whether or not the piece of wood involved is in fact northern oak or southern pine, or something else. Thus everyone theorizes.

Gillin's example indicates, of course, not only that Doakes is a practical theorist but that he employs various methods to test his theory as well. This is seen by Doakes using one or another procedure for verifying or validating his conclusion regarding the quality of the wood in which he has tried to hammer a nail. As I have stated earlier, then, we are all theorists who are constantly involved in utilizing various methodological procedures in investigations to test our theories. This is true for sociologists and laymen alike. As Gouldner (1970:496) points out: "There is not as great a difference between the sociologist and those he studies as the sociologist seems to think, even with respect to an intellectual interest in knowing social worlds. Those being studied are also avid students of human relations; they too have their social theories and conduct their investigations."

Thus, even though most sociologists are unable or unwilling to acknowledge the fact, there is at present a considerable admixture of these sociological specialties in the everyday activities of the great majority of sociologists. To pretend that this is not the case is both foolish and detrimental to the future of sociology. As one way of dealing with this problem, I have suggested that the sociological researcher should, as much as possible, make explicit his theories of behavior, models of men, and assumptions that guide, and, to a large extent, probably determine the outcome of his research activities. While it is more difficult to suggest what the theorist might do with regard to this issue, he should certainly be encouraged to be more self-conscious and open in revealing how his theories have arisen from his own personal experience and the various ways in which he has tested them prior to their arrival on the printed page.

Not only do all sociologists utilize an admixture of theories and methods in their own work but, equally important, they all assume one or another type of *theoretic actor* who knows what he is doing. As Shwayder (1965) points out, before one can theorize one must have practical knowledge. This is as true for the theoretic actor who is the object of each sociologist's concern as for the sociologist himself. We, as sociologists, presuppose that the objects of our sociological interest possess the practical knowledge of an ordinary societal member. Depending on our view of the ordinary societal member, we attribute certain theorizing and testing abilities to our research subjects. That is, like ourselves, we see them as acting on the basis of various theoretic notions and utilizing a variety of methodological procedures to test their notions. In other words, every sociologist has one or more models of man that guide his research, and, at the same time, he assumes one or another model of man on the part of those who are the object of his inquiry.

One thing that any investigator's data show us, therefore, is his formulation of a type of person. Or, to put it somewhat differently, a sociologist's utilization of one or another data-collection procedure has the important consequence of showing us the methods of that particular sociologist. From this point of view, what is most important about a sociological researcher's use of one or another procedure is whether or not his methods are explicit and reproductive. That is, he must try to provide explicit rules for allowing us to see how he has assembled what he knows.

This is true whatever sociological devices the sociologist employs: interviews, questionnaires, various types of participation and observational procedures, laboratory experiments, introspection, experimental designs in survey settings, unobtrusive measures, or historical documents. There are undoubtedly many advantages in using some of these techniques in combination, employing a series of complementary methods to collect sociological data. But the problem remains: the researcher still should strive *to provide the reader with the explicit rules by which he generates his conclusions.*

Different sociologists will, of course, offer different rules for their readers: theories, assumptions, methods, models of man. But one would hope that such attempts would lead some sociologists to offer a model of the actor that will guide us *in conducting our research.* As Cicourel (1964:61) puts it:

> If it is correct to assume that persons in everyday life order their environment, assign meanings or relevances to subjects, base their social actions on their common-sense rationalities, then one cannot engage in field research or use

any other method of research in the social sciences without taking the principle of subjective interpretation into consideration.

Many sociological investigations have, of course, had as one of their goals, the discovery of certain rules of subjective interpretation that would help us construct a model of the actor. A problem with these studies is that they have focused so narrowly on their empirical *results* that they have largely ignored the possible importance of the data-collection *process* itself as a source of data. To repeat what has been stated previously: sociologists must study the processes by which sociological data are obtained.

Sociological researchers must begin to recognize what they bring with them to the design, execution, and analysis of their investigations. We simply cannot afford to continue to engage in the same kinds of sterile, unproductive, unimaginative investigations which have long characterized most sociological research. A "science" (even if it is a *social* science) that contains few valid generalizations about human behavior and interaction that can be supported by empirical results, and that fails to achieve understanding because it studiously avoids the direct observation of behavior itself is scarcely deserving of its claim to scientific status.

References

Abrahamson, J. H.
1966 "Emotional disorder, status inconsistency, and migration." Milbank Memorial Fund Quarterly 44:23–48.

Adler, Ruth (ed.)
1970 The Working Press. New York: Bantam Books.

Athey, K. R.
1960 "Two experiments showing the effects of the interviewer's racial background on responses to questionnaires concerning racial issues." Journal of Applied Psychology 44:244–246.

Bakan, David
1967 On Method. San Francisco: Jossey-Bass.

Ball, John
1967 "The reliability and validity of interview data obtained from 59 narcotic drug addicts." American Journal of Sociology 72:650–654.

Barber, Theodore X., and Maurice J. Silver
1968a "Fact, fiction, and the experimenter bias effect." Psychological Bulletin Monograph 70:1–29.
1968b "Pitfalls in data analysis and interpretation: a reply to Rosenthal." Psychological Bulletin Monograph 70:48–62.

Barnlund, Dean C. (ed.)
1968 Interpersonal Communication: Survey and Studies. Boston: Houghton Mifflin.

Bass, B. M.
1955 "Authoritarianism or acquiescense?" Journal of Abnormal and Social Psychology 51:616–623.

Becker, Howard S.
1951 "The professional dance musician and his audience." American Journal of Sociology 57:136–154.
1958 "Problems of inference and proof in participant observation." American Sociological Review 23:652–660.
1963 Outsiders. New York: Free Press.

Bell, Charles G., and William Buchanan
1966 "Reliable and unreliable respondents: party registration and prestige pressure." Western Political Quarterly 29:37–43.

Benney, Mark, David Riesman, and Shirley A. Star
1956 "Age and sex in the interview." American Journal of Sociology 62: 143–152.

Berelson, Bernard, and Gary A. Steiner
1964   Human Behavior: An Inventory of Scientific Findings. New York: Harcourt, Brace & World.

Berger, Peter L.
1963   Invitation to Sociology: A Humanistic Perspective. New York: Doubleday Anchor.

Berger, Peter L., and Thomas Luckmann
1966   The Social Construction of Reality: A Treatise in the Sociology of Knowledge. Garden City, N.Y.: Doubleday.

Bierstedt, Robert
1963   The Social Order: An Introduction to Sociology. New York: McGraw-Hill.

Binder, A., D. McConnell, and Nancy A. Sjoholm
1957   "Verbal conditioning as a function of experimenter characteristics." Journal of Abnormal and Social Psychology 55:309–314.

Birdwhistell, Raymond I.
1952   Introduction to Kinesics. Washington: Foreign Service Institute.
1960   "Kinesics and communication." In R. Carpenter and M. McLuhan (eds.), Explorations in Communication. New York: Beacon Press.
1969   Remarks made at conference on "Film in Anthropological Teaching." New York University, October.

Blalock, Hubert M.
1968   "Theory building and causal inference." In Hubert M. Blalock and Ann B. Blalock (eds.), Methodology in Social Research, pp. 155–198. New York: McGraw-Hill.

1969a   "Comments on Coleman's paper." In Robert Bierstedt (ed.), A Design for Sociology: Scope, Objectives, and Methods, pp. 115–121. Philadelphia: American Academy of Political and Social Science.
1969b   "On graduate methodology training." American Sociologist 4:5–6.

Blau, Peter M.
1964   Exchange and Power in Social Life. New York: Wiley.

Blum, Alan F.
1969   "Methods for the study of social problems." Unpublished manuscript.

Blumer, Herbert
1954   "What is wrong with social theory?" American Sociological Review 19:3–10.
1956   "Sociological analysis and the 'variable'." American Sociological Review 21:683–690.
1962   "Society as social interaction." In Arnold M. Rose (ed.), Human Behavior and Social Processes: an Interactionist Approach, pp. 179–192. Boston: Houghton Mifflin.
1966   "Sociological implications of the thought of George Herbert Mead." American Journal of Sociology 71:535–544.

Bonjean, Charles M., Richard J. Hill, and S. Dale McLemore
1967   Sociological Measurement. San Francisco: Chandler.

Borgatta, Edgar F.
1969   "Some notes on graduate education, with special reference to sociology." American Sociologist 4:6–12.

Bradburn, Norman M., and David Caplovitz
1965   Reports on Happiness. Chicago: Aldine.

Bramson, Leon
1961   The Political Context of Sociology. Princeton, N.J.: Princeton University Press.

Breslin, Jimmy
1969   The World of Jimmy Breslin. New York: Ballantine Books.

Brookover, Wilbur B., and John B. Holland
1952   "An inquiry into the meaning of minority group attitude expression." American Sociological Review 17:196–202.

Brown, J. M.
1955   "Respondents rate public opinion interviewers." Journal of Applied Psychology 39:96–102.

Brown, Julia, and Brian G. Gilmartin
1969   "Sociology today: lacunae, emphases, and surfeits." American Sociologist 4:283–291.

Cahalan, Don
1968   "Correlates of respondent accuracy in the Denver validity survey." Public Opinion Quarterly 32:607–621.

Campbell, Angus, P. E. Converse, and W. E. Miller
1960   The American Voter. New York: Wiley.

Campbell, Donald T., and D. W. Fiske
1959   "Convergent and discriminant validation by the multitrait-multimethod matrix." Psychological Bulletin 56:81–105.

Cannell, Charles F., and Floyd J. Fowler
1963   "Comparison of a self-enumerative procedure and a personal interview: a validity study." Public Opinion Quarterly 27:250–264.
1964   "A note on interviewer effect in self-enumerative procedures." American Sociological Review 24:270.

Cannell, Charles F., Floyd J. Fowler, and Kent H. Marquis
1968   "The influence of interviewer and respondent psychological and behavioral variables on the reporting of household interviews." Vital and Health Statistics, Series 2, No. 26.

Cannell, Charles F., and Robert L. Kahn
1968   "Interviewing." In Gardner Lindzey and Eliot Aronson (eds.), The Handbook of Social Psychology. Vol. II, pp. 526–595. Reading, Mass.: Addison-Wesley.

Carmichael, L., S. Roberts, and N. Wessell.
1937   "A study of the judgment of manual expression as presented in still and motion pictures." Journal of Social Psychology 8:115–142.

Caudill, William
1958   The Psychiatric Hospital as a Small Society. Cambridge: Harvard University Press.

Chomsky, Noam
1969   American Power and the New Mandarins. New York: Vintage.

Cicourel, Aaron V.
1964   Method and Measurement in Sociology. New York: Free Press.

Clark, John P., and Larry L. Tifft
1966 "Polygraph and interview validation of self-reported deviant behavior." American Sociological Review 31:516–523.

Clausen, Aage R.
1968 "Response validity: vote report." Public Opinion Quarterly 32:588–606.

Cleveland, S.
1951 "The relationship between examiner anxiety and subjects' Rorschach scores." Microfilm Abstracts 11:415–416.

Coleman, James S.
1969 "The methods of sociology." In Robert Bierstedt (ed.), A Design for Sociology: Scope, Objectives, and Methods, pp. 86–114. Philadelphia: American Academy of Political and Social Science.

Cook, Stuart W., and Claire Selltiz
1964 "A multiple-indicator approach to attitude measurement." Psychological Bulletin 62:36–55.

Couch, Arthur, and Kenneth Keniston
1960 "Yeasayers and naysayers: agreeing response set as a personality variable." Journal of Abnormal and Social Psychology 60:151–174.

Crowne, D. P., and D. Marlowe
1964 The Approval Motive. New York: Wiley.

Cumming, Elaine, and John Cumming
1957 Closed Ranks: An Experiment in Mental Health Education. Cambridge: Harvard University Press.

Dalton, Melville
1959 Men Who Manage. New York: Wiley.

Davitz, J. R.
1964 The Communication of Emotional Meanings. New York: McGraw-Hill.

Davitz, J. R., and L. Davitz
1959 "The communication of feelings by content-free speech." Journal of Communication 9:110–117.

Dean, Lois
1958 "Interaction, reported and observed: the case of one local union." Human Organization 17:36–44.

DeFleur, Melvin L., and Frank R. Westie
1958 "Verbal attitudes and overt acts: an experiment in the salience of attitudes." American Sociological Review 23:667–673.

DeFriese, Gordon H., and W. Scott Ford
1969 "Verbal attitudes, overt acts, and the influence of social constraint in interracial behavior." Social Problems 16:493–505.

Denzin, Norman K.
1970 The Research Act. Chicago: Aldine.

Deutscher, Irwin
1966 "Word and deeds: social science and social policy." Social Problems 13:235–254.
1968 "Asking questions cross-culturally: some problems of linguistic

comparability." In Howard S. Becker et al. (eds.), Institutions nd the Person, pp. 318–341. Chicago: Aldine.
1969 "Looking backward: case studies on the progress of methodology in sociological research." American Sociologist 4:35–41.

Diamond, Edwin
1970 "The cabal at the 'New York Times': which way to the revolution?" New York Magazine 3:42–45.

Dohrenwend, Barbara S.
1969 "Comments on interviewer biasing effects: toward a reconsideration of findings." Public Opinion Quarterly 33:121–125.

Dohrenwend, Barbara S., John Colombotos, and Bruce P. Dohrenwend
1968 "Social distance and interviewer effects." Public Opinion Quarterly 32:410–422.

Dohrenwend, Bruce P.
1966 "Social status and psychological disorder: an issue of substance and an issue of method." American Sociological Review 31:14–34.

Dohrenwend, Bruce P., Viola W. Bernard, and Lawrence C. Kolb
1962 "The orientations of leaders in an urban area toward problems of mental illness." American Journal of Psychiatry 118:683–691.

Douglas, Jack D.
1970 The Relevance of Sociology. New York: Appleton-Century-Crofts.

Eckman, P.
1964 "Body position, facial expression, and verbal behavior during interviews." Journal of Abnormal and Social Psychology 68:295–301.

Edwards, E. L.
1959 "Social desirability and personality test construction." In B. M. Bass and I. A. Berg (eds.), Objective Approaches to Psychology, pp. 101–116. New York: Van Nostrand.

Efron, D.
1941 Gesture and Environment. New York: Kings Crown Press.

Ehrlich, Howard J.
1969 "Attitudes, behavior, and the intervening variables." American Sociology 4:29–34.

Ehrlich, June, and David Riesman
1961 "Age and authority in the interview." Public Opinion Quarterly 23:39–56.

Erikson, Kai T.
1962 "Notes on the sociology of deviance." Social Problems 9:307–314.

Etzioni, Amatai
1968 "Basic human needs, alienation, and inauthenticity." American Sociological Review 33:870–885.

Exley, Frederick
1969 A Fan's Notes. New York: Ballantine Books.

Exline, R.
1963 "Explorations in the process of person perception: visual inter-

action in relation to competition, sex and need for affiliation." Journal of Personality 31:1–20.

Exline, R., David Gray, and Dorothy Schuette
1965   "Visual behavior in a dyad as affected by interview content and sex of respondent." Journal of Personality and Social Psychology 1:201–209.

Fairbanks, G., and W. Pronovost
1939   "An experimental study of the pitch characteristics of the voice during the expression of emotion." Speech Monographs 6:87–104.

Festinger, Leon, Henry W. Riecken, and Stanley Schacter
1956   When Prophecy Fails. Minneapolis: University of Minnesota Press.

Finney, D. J.
1960   The Theory of Experimental Design. Chicago: University of Chicago Press.

Freedman, Ronald, Pascal Whelpton, and Arthur Campbell
1959   Family Planning, Sterility, and Population Growth. New York: McGraw-Hill.

Freeman, Linton C., and Turkoz Ataov
1960   "Invalidity of indirect and direct measures toward cheating." Journal of Personality 28:443–447.

Friedman, Neil
1967   The Social Nature of Psychological Research. New York: Basic Books.

Galtung, Johan
1967   Theory and Methods of Social Research. New York: Columbia University Press.

Gans, Herbert J.
1962   The Urban Villagers. Glencoe, Ill.: Free Press.
1967   The Levittowners. New York: Atheneum.
1968   "The participant-observer as a human being: observations on the personal aspects of field work." In Howard S. Becker et al. (eds.), Institutions and the Person, pp. 300–317. Chicago: Aldine.

Garfinkel, Harold
1967   Studies in Ethnomethodology. Englewood Cliffs, N.J.: Prentice-Hall.

Gerth, Hans H., and C. Wright Mills
1960   From Max Weber: Essays in Sociology. New York: Oxford University Press.

Gibson, J. J., and A. D. Pick
1963   "Perception of another person's looking behavior." American Journal of Psychology 76:86–94.

Gillin, John (ed.)
1954   For a Science of Social Man: Convergences in Anthropology, Psychology, and Sociology. New York: Macmillan.

Glaser, Barney, and Anselm Strauss
1965   "Discovery of substantive theory: a basic strategy underlying qualitative research." American Behavioral Scientist 8:5–11.

1967   The Discovery of Grounded Theory. Chicago: Aldine.
Glazer, Nathan
1967   "The ideological uses of sociology." In Paul F. Lazarsfeld, William
        H. Sewell, and Harold L. Wilensky (eds.), The Uses of Sociology,
        pp. 63–77. New York: Basic Books.
Goffman, Erving
1959   The Presentation of Self in Everyday Life. Garden City, N.Y.:
        Doubleday Anchor.
1963   Behavior in Public Places. New York: Free Press.
1967   Interaction Ritual. Garden City, N.Y.: Doubleday Anchor.
1969   Strategic Interaction. Philadelphia: University of Pennsylvania
        Press.
Gold, Raymond L.
1958   "Roles in sociological field observations." Social Forces 00.217–
        223.
Goode, William J., and Paul K. Hatt
1952   Methods in Social Research. New York: McGraw-Hill.
Goodmen, Norman, Stephen Richardson, Stanford Dornbusch, and Allen
        Hastorf
1963   "Variant reactions to physical disability." American Sociological
        Review 28:429–435.
Gordon, Raymond L.
1969   Interviewing: Strategy, Techniques, and Tactics. Homewood, III.:
        Dorsey Press.
Gould, Leroy C.
1969   "Who defines delinquency: a comparison of self-reported and
        officially reported indices of delinquency for three racial groups."
        Social Problems 16:325–336.
Gouldner, Alvin W.
1959   "Reciprocity and autonomy in functional theory." In L. Gross (ed.),
        Symposium on Sociological Theory. New York: Row, Peterson.
1970   The Coming Crisis in Western Sociology. New York: Basic Books.
Green, Bert F.
1954   "Attitude measurement." In Gardner Lindzey (ed.), Handbook of
        Social Psychology. Vol. I, pp. 335–369. Reading, Mass.: Addison-
        Wesley.
Green, Lawrence W.
1969   "East Pakistan: knowledge and use of contraceptives." Studies in
        Family Planning 39:9–14.
Greer, Scott
1969   The Logic of Social Inquiry. Chicago: Aldine.
Gurin, Gerald, Joseph Veroff, and Sheila Feld
1960   Americans View Their Mental Health. New York: Basic Books.
Haberman, Paul W.
1963   "The use of a psychological test for recall of past situations."
        Journal of Clinical Psychology 19:245–248.
Hall, Edward T.
1969a   The Silent Language. Garden City, N.Y.: Doubleday Anchor.

1969b The Hidden Dimension. Garden City, N.Y.: Doubleday Anchor.
Hamblin, Robert L.
1966 "Ratio measurement and sociological theory." Department of
Sociology. Washington University, St. Louis, mimeographed.
Hambright, Thea Zelman
1969 "Comparison of information on death certificates and matching
1960 census records: age, marital status, race, nativity, and country of origin." Demography 6:413–423.
Hammond, Phillip E. (ed.)
1964 Sociologists at Work. New York: Basic Books.
Harvey, S. M.
1938 "Preliminary investigation of the interview." British Journal of
Psychology 28:263–287.
Hassinger, Edward, and Robert L. McNamara
1957 "Stated opinion and actual practice in health behavior in a rural
area." The Midwest Sociologist: 93–97.
Hauser, Philip
1969 "Comments on Coleman's paper." In Robert Bierstedt (ed.), A
Design for Sociology: Scope, Objectives, and Methods, pp. 122–
136. Philadelphia: American Academy of Political and Social
Science.
Heilbrun, Alfred B.
1964 "Social learning theory, social desirability, and the MMPI." Psy-
chological Bulletin 61:377–387.
Hill, Richard J.
1969 "On the relevance of methodology." et al. 2:26–29.
Holzner, Burkhart
1968 Reality Construction in Society. Cambridge, Mass.: Schenkman.
Homans, George C.
1961 Social Behavior: Its Elementary Forms. New York: Harcourt, Brace
& World.
1964 "Contemporary theory in sociology." In Robert E. L. Faris (ed.),
Handbook of Modern Sociology, pp. 951–977. Chicago: Rand
McNally.
1967 The Nature of Social Science. New York: Harcourt, Brace & World.
Hughes, H. Stuart
1961 Consciousness and Society. New York: Random House.
Hyman, Herbert
1949 "Inconsistencies as a problem of attitude measurement." Journal
of Social Issues 5:40–41.
1954 Interviewing in Social Research. Chicago: University of Chicago
Press.
Jaco, E. Gartly
1960 The Social Epidemiology of Mental Disorders. New York: Russell
Sage Foundation.
Jacobs, Jane
1961 The Death and Life of Great American Cities. New York: Random
House.

James, W.
1932   "A study of the expression of bodily posture." Journal of General Psychology 7:405–436.

Kaplan, Abraham
1964   The Conduct of Inquiry. San Francisco: Chandler.

Katona, George
1960   The Powerful Consumer. New York: McGraw-Hill.

Katz, D.
1942   "Do interviewers bias poll results?" Public Opinion Quarterly 6:248–268.

Katz, Irwin
1964   "Body language: a study in unintended communication." Unpublished doctoral dissertation, Harvard University.

Kaufman, Felix
1958   Methodology of the Social Sciences. New York: Humanities Press.

Kinsey, Alfred C., Warden B. Pomeroy, and Clyde E. Martin
1948   Sexual Behavior in the Human Male. Philadelphia: W. B. Saunders.

Kish, Leslie
1959   "Some statistical problems in research design." American Sociological Review 24:328–338.

Kitsuse, John I.
1964   "Societal reaction to deviant behavior: problems of theory and method." In Howard S. Becker (ed.), The Other Side. New York: Free Press.

Kuhn, Thomas S.
1962   The Structure of Scientific Revolutions. Chicago: University of Chicago Press.

Kutner, B., C. Wilkins, and P. Yarrow
1952   "Verbal attitudes and overt behavior involving racial prejudice." Journal of Abnormal and Social Psychology 47:649–652.

Laing, Ronald D.
1967   The Politics of Experience. New York: Ballantine Books.

Laing, Ronald D., H. Phillipson, and A. R. Lee
1966   Interpersonal Perception: A Theory and a Method of Research. London: Tavistock Publications.

Langner, Thomas S., and Stanley T. Michael
1963   Life Stress and Mental Health. New York: Free Press.

LaPiere, Richard T.
1934   "Attitudes vs. actions." Social Forces 13:230–237.
1969   "Comment on Irwin Deutscher's look backward." American Sociologist 4:41–42.

Larsen, Otto, and Melvin DeFleur
1955   "Validity and reliability in measurement of message diffusion." Proceedings of Pacific Sociological Society, pp. 110–120.

Lazarsfeld, Paul F., William H. Sewell, and Harold L. Wilensky (eds.)
1967   The Uses of Sociology. New York: Basic Books.

Lehmann-Haupt, Christopher
1969   "Thoughts for the end of the year." The New York Times, December 31.

Leighton, Alexander
1959   My Name Is Legion. New York: Basic Books.

Leighton, Dorothea, John S. Harding, David B. Macklin, Allister M. Mac-Millan, and Alexander H. Leighton
1963   The Character of Danger. New York: Basic Books.

Lemert, Edwin M.
1951   Social Pathology. New York: McGraw-Hill.
1967   Human Deviance, Social Problems and Social Control. Englewood Cliffs, N.J.: Prentice-Hall.

Lemkau, Paul V., and Guido M. Crocetti
1962   "An urban population's opinion and knowledge about mental illness." The American Journal of Psychiatry 118:692–700.

Lenski, Gerhard
1963   The Religious Factor. New York: Anchor Books Edition.
1966   Power and Privilege. New York: McGraw-Hill.

Lenski, Gerhard, and John C. Leggett
1960   "Caste, class, and deference in the research interview." American Journal of Sociology 65:463–467.

Liebow, Elliot
1968   Tally's Corner. Boston: Little, Brown.

Lindquist, E. F.
1953   Design of Experiments in Psychology and Education. Boston: Houghton Mifflin.

Linn, Lawrence S.
1965   "Verbal attitudes and overt behavior: a study of racial discrimination." Social Forces 43:353–364.

Linton, Ralph
1945   The Cultural Background of Personality. New York: Appleton-Century-Crofts.

Lohman, Joseph, and D. Reitzes
1954   "Deliberately organized groups and racial behavior." American Sociological Review 19:342–348.

Lowen, A.
1958   Physical Dynamics of Character Structure. New York: Grune and Stratton.

Luft, J.
1953   "Interaction and projection." Journal of Projective Techniques 17:489–492.

Lynd, Robert S.
1964   Knowledge for What? New York: Grove Press Edition.

Lynd, Staughton
1968   "A profession of history." New American Review, No. 2, pp. 192–205. New York: New American Library.

Maccoby, Eleanor, and Nathan Maccoby
1954   "The interview: a tool of social science." In Gardner Lindzey (ed.),
       Handbook of Social Psychology. Vol. I. Reading, Mass.: Addison-
       Wesley.

Maddox, George L., Kurt W. Back, and Veronica R. Liederman
1968   "Overweight as social deviance and disability." Journal of Health
       and Social Behavior 4:287–298.

Mailer, Norman
1968   The Idol and the Octopus. New York: Dell.

Manis, Jerome C., Milton J. Brawer, Chester L. Hunt, and Leonard C.
       Kercher
1964   "Estimating the prevalence of mental illness." American Socio-
       logical Review 29:84–89.

Mannheim, Karl
1957   Systematic Sociology. New York: Grove Press.

Maslow, Abraham
1966   The Psychology of Science. New York: Harper & Row.

Maslow, Abraham, and N. Mintz
1956   "Effects of esthetic surroundings: I. initial effects of three esthetic
       conditions upon perceiving 'energy' and 'well-being' in faces."
       Journal of Psychology 41:247–254.

McCall, George J., and J. L. Simmons
1969   Issues in Participant Observation. Reading, Mass.: Addison-
       Wesley.

McGuigan, Frank J.
1963   "The experimenter: a neglected stimulus object." Psychological
       Bulletin 60:421–428.

Menzel, Herbert
1968   Personal written communication.

Merton, Robert K.
1957   Social Theory and Social Structure. New York: Free Press.

Messick, Samuel, and Douglas N. Jackson
1961   "Desirability scale values and dispersions for MMPI." Psycho-
       logical Reports 8:409–414.

Milgram, Stanley
1969   "The lost letter technique." Psychology Today 3:30–33.
1970   "The experience of living in cities." Science 167:1461–1468.

Milgram, Stanley, Leon Mann, and Susan Harter
1965   "The lost letter technique: a tool of social research." Public Opin-
       ion Quarterly 29:437–438.

Mills, C. Wright
1940a "Methodological consequences of the sociology of knowledge."
       American Sociological Review 5:316–330.
1940b "Situated actions and vocabularies of motive." American Socio-
       logical Review 5:904–913.

Mintz, N.
1956   "Effects of esthetic surroundings: II. prolonged and repeated

experience in a 'beautiful' and an 'ugly' room." Journal of Psychology 41:459–466.

Moore, Omar K., and Alan R. Anderson
1965   "Puzzles, games, and social interaction." In David Braybrooke (ed.), Philosophical Problems of the Social Sciences, pp. 68–79. New York: Macmillan.

Morris, Willie
1970   "Yazoo: notes on survival." Harper's 240:43–70.

Mulry, R. C.
1962   "The effects of the experimenter's perception of his own performance on subject performance in a pursuit rotor task." Unpublished master's thesis, University of North Dakota.

Myrdal, Gunnar
1969   Objectivity in Social Research. New York: Pantheon.

Nathanson, Maurice
1963   Philosophy of the Social Sciences: A Reader. New York: Random House.
1970   The Journeying Self: A Study in Philosophy and Social Role. Reading. Mass.: Addison-Wesley.

Newfield, Jack
1970   Robert Kennedy: A Memoir. New York: Bantam Books.

New York Times
1969   "How to succeed in the census-taking business." December 23, p. 53.

Nicolaus, Martin
1969   "Remarks at ASA convention." American Sociologist 4:154–156.

Nielson, G.
1962   Studies in Self-Confrontation. Copenhagen: Munksgaard.

Nisbet, Robert
1970   "Subjective si! objective no!" The New York Times Book Review. April 5:1–2, 36–37.

Nunnally, Jum C.
1967   Psychometric Theory. New York: McGraw-Hill.

Parry, Hugh, and Helen M. Crossley
1950   "Validity of responses to survey questions." Public Opinion Quarterly 14:61–80.

Parsons, Talcott
1937   The Structure of Social Action. New York: McGraw-Hill.
1951   The Social System. New York: Free Press.

Phillips, Derek L.
1963   "Rejection: a possible consequence of seeking help for mental disorders." American Sociological Review 28:963–972.
1965   Studies in American Society. New York: Thomas Y. Crowell.
1966   "The 'true prevalence' of mental illness in a New England state." Community Mental Health Journal 2:35–40.
1967a   "Social participation and happiness." American Journal of Sociology 72:479–488.

1967b   Studies in American Society: II. New York: Thomas Y. Crowell.
Phillips, Derek L., and Kevin J. Clancy
1970   "Response biases in field studies of mental illness." American Sociological Review 35:503–515.
Phillips, Derek L., and Bernard E. Segal
1969   "Sexual status and psychiatric symptoms." American Sociological Review 34:58–72.
Phillips, Derek L., and Thomas P. Wilson
1967   "Applications of experimental designs in survey settings." Sociological Inquiry 39:333–339.
Polanyi, Michael
1964   Personal Knowledge: Towards a Post-Critical Philosophy. New York: Harper & Row.
Putney, Snell, and Russell Middleton
1962   "Ethical relativism and anomia." American Journal of Sociology 67:430–438.
Rankin, R., and Donald T. Campbell
1955   "Galvanic skin response to Negro and white experimenters." Journal of Abnormal and Social Psychology 51:30–33.
Redfield, Robert
1948   "The art of social science." American Journal of Sociology 55:181–190.
Reiss, Albert J.
1968   "Stuff and nonsense about social surveys and observation." In Howard S. Becker et al. (eds.), Institutions and the Person, pp. 351–367. Chicago: Aldine.
Rice, Stuart A.
1929   "Contagious bias in the interview: a methodological note." American Journal of Sociology 35:420–423.
Richardson, Stephen, Barbara S. Dohrenwend, and David Klein
1965   Interviewing: Its Forms and Functions. New York: Basic Books.
Richardson, Stephen, Norman Goodman, Allen Hastorf, and Stanford Dornbusch
1961   "Cultural uniformity and reaction to physical disability." American Sociological Review 26:241–247.
Riecken, Henry W.
1962   "A program for research on experiments in social psychology." In N. F. Washburne (ed.), Decisions, Values, and Groups. Vol. 2, pp. 25–41. New York: Pergamon.
Riesman, David
1958   "Interviewers, elites, and academic freedom." Social Problems 6:115–126.
Riley, Matilda White
1963   Sociological Research I: A Case Approach. New York: Harcourt, Brace & World.
Robins, Lee N.
1963   "The reluctant respondent." Public Opinion Quarterly 27:276–286.

Robinson, J., and S. Rohde
1946 "Two experiments with an anti-Semitism poll." Journal of Ab-
      normal and Social Psychology 41:136–144.

Rorer, Leonard G.
1965 "The great response-style myth." Psychological Bulletin 3:129–
      156.

Rosenberg, Milton J.
1965 "When dissonance fails: on eliminating evaluation apprehension
      from attitude measurement." Journal of Personality and Social
      Psychology 1:28–42.
1969 "The conditions and consequences of evaluation apprehension."
      In Robert Rosenthal and R. Rosnow (eds.), Artifact in Behavioral
      Research. New York: Academic Press.

Rosenthal, Robert
1966 Experimenter Effects in Behavioral Research. New York: Apple-
      ton-Century-Crofts.
1968 "Experimenter expectancy and the reassuring nature of the null
      hypothesis decision procedure." Psychological Bulletin Mono-
      graph 70:30–47.

Rosenthal, Robert, and K. Fode
1963 "Psychology of the scientist: V. three experiments in experimenter
      bias." Psychological Reports 12:491–511.

Rosten, Leo
1970 The Joys of Yiddish. New York: Pocket Books.

Roszak, Theodore
1969 The Making of a Counter Culture. Garden City, N.Y.: Doubleday
      Anchor.

Roth, Julius A.
1963 Timetables. New York: Bobbs-Merrill.

Ruesch, J., and W. Kees
1956 Nonverbal Communication: Notes on the Visual Perception of
      Human Relations. Berkeley: University of California Press.

Saarinen, E.
1948 The Search for Form. New York: Reinhold.

Saenger, Gerhart, and Emily Gilbert
1950 "Customer reactions to the integration of Negro sales personnel."
      International Journal of Opinion and Attitude Research 4:57–76.

Sampson, E. E., and J. R. F. French
1960 "An experiment on active and passive resistance to social power."
      American Psychologist 15:396 (Abstract).

Sarason, I. G.
1962 "Individual differences, situational variables, and personality re-
      search." Journal of Abnormal and Social Psychology 65:376–380.

Sarason, I. G., and M. Harmatz
1965 "Test anxiety and experimenter condition." Journal of Personality
      and Social Psychology 1:499–505.

Sartre, Jean-Paul
  1956   Being and Nothingness: An Essay on Phenomenological Ontology.
         Translated with an introduction by Hazel E. Barnes. New York:
         Philosophical Library.

Scheff, Thomas J.
  1966   Being Mentally Ill. Chicago: Aldine.

Schutz, Alfred
  1953   "Common-sense and scientific interpretations of human actions."
         Philosophy and Phenomenological Research 14:1–37.
  1954   "Concept and theory formation in the social sciences." The Jour-
         nal of Philosophy LI:257–273.

Schwartz, Morris S., and Charlotte G. Schwartz
  1955   "Problems in participant observation." American Journal of Soci-
         ology 60:343–354.

Sechrest, Lee
  1968   "Testing, measuring, and assessing people." In Edgar F. Borgatta
         and William W. Lambert (eds.), Handbook of Personality Theory
         and Research, pp. 529–628. Chicago: Rand McNally.

Selltiz, Claire, Marie Jahoda, Morton Deutsch, and Stuart W. Cook
  1959   Research Methods in Social Relations. Rev. ed. New York: Holt,
         Rinehart & Winston.

Shwayder, D. S.
  1965   The Stratification of Behavior. New York: Humanities Press.

Simmel, Georg
  1921   "Sociology of the senses: visual interaction." In R. Park and E.
         Burgess (eds.), Introduction to the Science of Sociology. Chicago:
         University of Chicago Press.

Sjoberg, Gideon, and Roger Nett
  1968   A Methodology for Social Research. New York: Harper & Row.

Smeiser, Neil J.
  1969   "The optimum scope of sociology." In Robert Bierstedt (ed.), A
         Design for Sociology: Scope, Objectives, and Methods, pp. 1–21.
         Philadelphia: American Academy of Political and Social Science.

Sommer, Robert
  1959   "Studies in personal space." Sociometry 22:247–260.
  1962   "The distance for comfortable conversation: a further study." So-
         ciometry 25:111–116.
  1965   "Further studies in small group ecology." Sociometry 28:337–348.
  1969   Personal Space: The Behavioral Basis of Design. Englewood
         Cliffs, N.J.: Prentice-Hall.

Sontag, Susan
  1969   "A letter from Sweden." Ramparts 8:23–38.

Srole, Leo, Thomas S. Langner, Stanley T. Michael, Marvin K. Opler, and
         Thomas A. C. Rennie
  1962   Mental Health in the Metropolis. New York: McGraw-Hill.

Star, Shirley
  1957   "The place of psychiatry in popular thinking." Paper read at the

meetings of the American Association for Public Opinion Research, Washington, D.C., May.

Steinzor, B.
1950   "The spatial factor in face to face discussion groups." Journal of Abnormal and Social Psychology 45:552–555.

Stevenson, H. W., and S. Allen
1964   "Adult performance as a function of the sex of experimenter and sex of subject." Journal of Abnormal and Social Psychology 68: 214–216.

Stevenson, H. W., and R. D. Odum
1963   "Visual reinforcement with children." Unpublished manuscript, University of Minnesota.

Storer, Norman W.
1966   The Social System of Science. New York: Holt, Rinehart & Winston.

Stouffer, Samuel A.
1950   "Some observations on study design." American Journal of Sociology 40:353–361.

Straus, Murray A.
1964   "Measuring families." In Harold T. Christensen (ed.), Handbook of Marriage and the Family, pp. 335–400. Chicago: Rand McNally.

Summers, Gene F.
1969   "Psychiatric symptoms and the use of rehabilitative facilities." Unpublished manuscript, University of Illinois.
1970   Attitude Measurement. Chicago: Rand McNally.

Summers, Gene F., and Andre D. Hammonds
1966   "Effect of racial characteristics of investigator on self-enumerated responses to a Negro prejudice scale." Social Forces 44:515–518.
1969   "Toward a paradigm for respondent bias in survey research." Sociological Quarterly 10:113–121.

Suttles, Gerald
1968   The Social Order of the Slum: Ethnicity and Territory in the Inner City. Chicago: University of Chicago Press.

Talese, Gay
1970   The Kingdom and the Power. New York: Bantam Books.

Tinbergen, Niko
1967   The Herring Gull's World. Garden City, N.Y.: Doubleday Anchor.

Tiryakian, Edward A.
1965   "Existential phenomenology." American Sociological Review 30: 674–678.

Turner, Ralph
1962   "Role-taking: process versus conformity." In Arnold M. Rose (ed.), Human Behavior and Social Process: An Interactionist Approach. Boston: Houghton Mifflin.

Vonnegut, Kurt Jr.
1969   Slaughterhouse-Five. New York: Dell.

Warriner, Charles F.
1958   "The nature and functions of official morality." American Journal of Sociology 64:165–168.

Watson, James D.
1968   The Double Helix. New York: Atheneum.

Webb, Eugene J., Donald T. Campbell, Richard D. Schwartz, and Lee Sechrest
1966   Unobtrusive Measures; Nonreactive Research in the Social Sciences. Chicago: Rand McNally.

Weber, Max
1947   The Theory of Social and Economic Organization. Trans. Talcott Parsons. New York: Oxford University Press.
1949   On the Methodology of the Social Sciences. Edward A. Shils (ed.), trans. Henry Finch. Glencoe, Ill.: Free Press.
1958   The Protestant Ethic and the Spirit of Capitalism. New York: Charles Scribner's Sons

Weick, Karl E.
1968   "Systematic observational methods." In Gardner Lindzey and Eliot Aronson (eds.), Handbook of Social Psychology. Vol. II, pp. 357–451. Reading, Mass.: Addison-Wesley.

Weiss, Carol
1968   "Validity of welfare mothers' interview responses." Public Opinion Quarterly 32:622–633.
1969   "Comments on interviewer biasing effects: toward a reconsideration of findings." Public Opinion Quarterly 33:127–129.

Weiss, Robert S.
1968   "Issues in holistic research." In Howard S. Becker et al. (eds.), Institutions and the Person, pp. 342–350. Chicago: Aldine.

Wells, William D.
1963   "How chronic overclaimers distort survey findings." Journal of Advertising Research 3:8–18.

Whyte, William F.
1955   Street Corner Society. Chicago: University of Chicago Press.
1969a   "Reflections on my work." In Irving Louis Horowitz (ed.), Sociological Self-Images, pp. 35–49. Beverly Hills, Calif.: Sage Publications.
1969b   "The role of the U.S. professor in developing countries." American Sociologist 4:19–28.

Whyte, William H.
1956   The Organization Man. New York: Simon & Schuster.

Williams, J. A., Jr.
1964   "Interviewing respondent interaction: a study of bias in the information interview." Sociometry 27:338–352.
1968   "Interviewer role performance: a further note on bias in the information interview." Public Opinion Quarterly 32:287–294.
1969   "Comments on interviewer biasing effects: toward a reconsideration of findings." Public Opinion Quarterly 33:125–127.

Williams, Robin W., Jr.
1969   "Comments on Smelser's paper." In Robert Bierstedt (ed.), A Design for Sociology: Scope, Objectives, and Methods, pp. 22–29. Philadelphia: American Academy of Political and Social Science.

Wilson, Thomas P.
1970   "Conceptions of interaction and forms of sociological explanation." American Sociological Review 35:697–710.

Winch, Peter
1967   The Idea of a Social Science. New York: Humanities Press.

Winkel, G. H., and I. G. Sarason
1964   "Subject, experimenter, and situational variables in research on anxiety." Journal of Abnormal and Social Psychology 68:601–608.

Wrong, Dennis H.
1961   "The over-socialized conception of man." American Sociological Review 26:185–193.

Wyatt, D. F., and Donald T. Campbell
1950   "A study of interviewer bias as related to interviewers' expectations and own opinions." International Journal of Opinion and Attitude Research 4:77–83.

Young, Pauline V.
1966   Scientific Social Surveys and Research. Englewood Cliffs. N.J.: Prentice-Hall.

Credits and Acknowledgments

I wish to express my thanks to the following publishers who have given permission to reprint from their publications:

To Academic Press, Inc., for Robert Rosenthal and R. Rosnow, *Artifact in Behavioral Research.*

To Addison-Wesley Publishing Company for *The Handbook of Social Psychology,* Volume II, Second edition, edited by Gardner Lindzey and Eliot Aronson, 1968, Addison-Wesley, Reading, Mass.; and for *The Journeying Self; A Study in Philosophy and Social Role* by Maurice Nathanson, 1970.

To Aldine Publishing Company for Howard S. Becker et al., *Institutions and the Person;* and Scott Greer, *The Logic of Social Inquiry.*

To the American Academy of Political and Social Science for *A Design for Sociology: Scope, Objectives, and Methods,* edited by Robert Bierstedt, Monograph 9.

To the American Psychological Association for P. Eckman, "Body Position, Facial Expression, and Verbal Behavior during Interviews," *Journal of Abnormal and Social Psychology,* 68, 1964, 295–301, copyright 1964 by the American Psychological Assn.; R. Exline, David Gray, and Dorothy Schuette, "Visual Behavior in a Dyad as Affected by Interview Content and Sex of Respondent," *Journal of Personality and Social Psychology,* 1, 1965, 201–209, copyright 1965 by the American Psychological Assn.; and Stuart W. Cook and Claire Selltiz, "A Multiple-Indicator Approach to Attitude Measurement," *Psychological Bulletin,* 62, 1964, 36–55, copyright 1964 by the American Psychological Assn., and all reprinted by permission.

To the American Sociological Association to reprint from *American Sociological Review:* John P. Clark and Larry L. Tifft, "Polygraph and Interview Validation of Self-reported Deviant Behavior," Bruce P. Dohrenwend, "Social Status and Psychological Disorder: An Issue of Substance and an Issue of Method," C. Wright Mills, "Methodological Consequences of the Sociology of Knowledge," and Thomas P. Wilson, "Conceptions of Interaction and Forms of Sociological Explanation"; from *American Sociologist:* Julia Brown and Brian G. Gilmartin, "Sociology Today: Lacunae, Emphases, and Surfeits," and Martin Nicolaus, "Remarks at ASA Convention"; and from *Sociometry:* Robert Sommer, "Further Studies in Small Group Ecology."

To Appleton-Century-Crofts, Inc., for Jack Douglas, *The Relevance of Sociology,* copyright 1970, Appleton-Century-Crofts, Educational Division, Meredith Corporation; and Robert Rosenthal, *Experimenter Effects in Behavioral Research,* copyright 1966, Appleton-Century-Crofts, Educational Division, Meredith Corporation.

To Basic Books, Inc., from *The Social Nature of Psychological Research* by Neil Friedman, Basic Books, Inc., Publishers, New York, 1967; from *The Coming Crisis in Western Sociology* by Alvin W. Gouldner, Basic Books, Inc., Publishers, New York, 1970; from *The Uses of Sociology,* edited by Paul F. Lazarsfeld, William H. Sewell, and Harold L. Wilensky, Basic Books, Inc., Publishers, New York, 1967; and from *Interviewing: Its Forms and Functions* by Stephen A. Richardson, Barbara Snell Dohrenwend, and David Klein, Basic Books, Inc., Publishers, New York, 1965.

To Alan F. Blum for his unpublished "Methods for the Study of Social Problems."

To Chandler Publishing Company for Charles M. Bonjean, Richard J. Hill, and S. Dale McLemore, *Sociological Measurement.*

To Communications/Research/Machines, Inc., for Stanley Milgram, "The Lost Letter Technique." in *Psychology Today.*

To Dorsey Press, Inc., for Raymond L. Gordon, *Interviewing: Strategy, Techniques, and Tactics.*

To Doubleday & Company, Inc., for *The Presentation of Self in Everyday Life,* by Erving Goffman, copyright 1959, Doubleday & Company, Inc.

To The Macmillan Company for Aaron V. Cicourel, *Method and Measurement in Sociology,* copyright © 1964 by The Free Press of Glencoe, a Division of The Macmillan Co.; Robert K. Merton, *Social Theory and Social Structure,* copyright 1957 by The Free Press, a corporation; Max Weber, *On the Methodology of the Social Sciences,* edited by Edward A. Shils, translated by Henry Finch, copyright 1949 by The Free Press; and Max Weber, *The Theory of Social and Economic Organization,* translated by Talcott Parsons, copyright 1947 by Talcott Parsons.

To the estate of John Gillin for the quotation from *For a Science of Social Man: Convergences in Anthropology, Psychology, and Sociology.*

To Grune & Stratton, Inc., Publishers, and Alexander Lowen, M.D., for *Physical Dynamics of Character Structure.*

To Robert L. Hamblin for his unpublished "Ratio Measurement and Sociological Theory."

To Harcourt Brace Jovanovich, Inc., for Bernard Berelson and Gary A. Steiner, *Human Behavior: An Inventory of Scientific Findings.*

To Harper & Row Publishers, Inc., for L. Gross, *Symposium on Sociological Theory;* and Abraham Maslow, *The Psychology of Science.*

To Harper's Magazine Company for Willie Morris, "Yazoo: Notes on Survival."

To Holt, Rinehart and Winston, Inc., for C. Selltiz, M. Jahoda, M. Deutsch, and S. W. Cook, *Research Methods in Social Relations,* revised edition.

To Houghton Mifflin Company for Dean C. Barnlund, *Interpersonal Communication: Survey and Studies.*

To Humanities Press, Inc., for Felix Kaufman, *Methodology of the Social Sciences,* and Peter Winch, *The Idea of a Social Science,* both published in New York by Humanities Press, Inc.

To Jossey-Bass Publishers, Inc., for David Bakan, *On Method.*

To the *Journal of Philosophy* for Alfred Schutz, "Concept and Theory Formation in the Social Sciences."

To McGraw-Hill Book Company for Robert Bierstedt, *The Social Order: An Introduction to Sociology;* and from *The Joys of Yiddish,* by Leo Rosten, copyright © 1968 by Leo Rosten, used with permission of McGraw-Hill Book Co.

To The Macmillan Company for David Braybrooke, *Philosophical Problems of the Social Sciences,* copyright © by David Braybrooke, 1965.

To Penguin Books, Ltd., for Ronald D. Laing, *The Politics of Experience.*

To Prentice-Hall, Inc., for Harold Garfinkel, *Studies in Ethnomethodology.*

To *Public Opinion Quarterly* for Carol Weiss, "Validity of Welfare Mothers' Interview Responses," published by Columbia University Press.

To Rand McNally & Company for Edgar F. Borgatta and William W. Lambert, *Handbook of Personality Theory and Research;* and Eugene J. Webb, Donald T. Campbell, Richard D. Schwartz, and Lee Secrest, *Unobtrusive Measures. Nonreactive Research in the Social Sciences.*

To Simon & Schuster, Inc., for William H. Whyte, *The Organization Man.*

To the Society for the Study of Social Problems and Leroy C. Gould for "Who Defines Delinquency: A Comparison of Self-reported and Officially Reported Indices of Delinquency for Three Racial Groups," from *Social Problems,* 1969.

To *The Sociological Quarterly* for Gene Summers and Andre Hammonds, "Toward a Paradigm for Respondent Bias in Survey Research," 10:1, 1969.

To the University of Chicago Press for Herbert Blumer, "Sociological Implications of the Thought of George Herbert Mead," *American Journal of Sociology,* 1966, 71:535–544, copyright © 1966 by University of Chicago Press; and Morris S. Schwartz and Charlotte Schwartz, "Problems in Participant Observation," *American Journal of Sociology,* 1955, 60: 343–354, copyright © 1955 by University of Chicago Press.

To John Wiley & Sons, Inc., for D. P. Crowne and D. Marlowe, *The Approval Motive.*

To The World Publishing Company for *The Kingdom and the Power,* by Gay Talese, an NAL book, copyright © 1969 by Gay Talese and used with permission of The World Publishing Company.

Index

Printed in U.S.A.